Presented To:

_____

From:

_____

Date:

_____

Look into the depths
OF ANOTHER'S SOUL
AND LISTEN,

not only with our ears,
BUT WITH OUR HEARTS
AND IMAGINATION,

and our silent love.

⟐ JOYE KANELAKOS ⟐

The Ultimate Gift

BY
JIM STOVALL

David C Cook

transforming lives together

THE ULTIMATE GIFT
Published by David C. Cook
4050 Lee Vance View
Colorado Springs, CO 80918 U.S.A.

David C. Cook Distribution Canada
55 Woodslee Avenue, Paris, Ontario, Canada N3L 3E5

David C. Cook U.K., Kingsway Communications
Eastbourne, East Sussex BN23 6NT, England

The Web site addresses recommended throughout this book are offered as
a resource to you. These Web sites are not intended in any way to be or imply
an endorsement on the part of David C. Cook, nor do we vouch for their content.

The characters and events in this book are fictional, and any
resemblance to actual persons or events is coincidental.

LCCN 2007931562
ISBN 978-0-7814-4563-4

Illustrations by Elise Peterson

Printed in Canada
First Edition 2007

1 2 3 4 5 6 7 8 9 10

062707

Introduction

You and I are preparing to take a journey together within the pages of this book that you hold in your hands. I want to thank you for the investment you have made and will be making in our journey.

I believe that when you read the last page of *The Ultimate Gift*, you will be a different person than you are at this moment. At that point, our journey together will have ended, but your journey into the fullness of your destiny will be just beginning.

Like any other journey or trip you have ever taken, it becomes more meaningful based upon the special people in your life who share this trip with you. I am sure you can remember wonderful trips or vacations that you have been on in the past. As those pleasant memories of your travels come back to you, they are filled not only with your destination, but the special people and loved ones who shared the journey with you.

When you have concluded reading *The Ultimate Gift* and have begun in earnest your life's journey, my fervent hope is that you will share *The Ultimate Gift* with friends, family, and the special people in your world who make your life's journey priceless.

Thank you for sharing this part of my life's journey and for allowing me and the *The Ultimate Gift* to travel with you on part of your life's journey.

Respectfully,
Jim Stovall

TABLE OF CONTENTS

ONE

In the Beginning

A journey may be long or short,
but it must start at the very spot
one finds oneself.

I t was in my fifty-third year of practicing law, and my eightieth year of life here on this earth, that I was to undertake an odyssey that would change my life forever.

I was seated behind my mahogany monstrosity of a desk in my top-floor, corner office of an imposing building in the most prominent section of Boston. In the marble foyer, the antique brass plate on the outer door reads Hamilton, Hamilton, & Hamilton. Of the aforementioned, I am the first Hamilton—Theodore J. Hamilton, to be accurate. My son and grandson account for the remainder of the Hamiltons in the firm.

I would not say that we are the most prestigious law firm in all of Boston, because that would not be totally circumspect. However, if someone else were to say that, I would not go out of my way to disagree.

As I was simply drinking in the ambiance in my antiquated but palatial office, I was thinking how far I had come since the lean days in law school. I enjoyed gazing upon my wall of fame, which includes photographs taken of me with the last five presidents of the United States, among other significant persons.

I glanced at the familiar sight of floor-to-ceiling shelves of leather-bound books, the massive oriental rug, and the classic leather furniture, all of which predate me. My enjoyment in simply experiencing the familiar environment was interrupted when the telephone on my desk buzzed. I heard the reliable and familiar voice of Margaret Hastings. "Sir," she said, "may I step in and have a word with you?"

As we had been working together for more than forty years, I knew that tone was reserved for the most serious and somber of circumstances.

"Come in, please," I replied immediately.

Miss Hastings entered promptly, securing the door behind her, and sat across the desk from me. She had not brought her calendar, her correspondence, or documents of any type. I was trying to remember the last time Margaret had entered my inner sanctum without some baggage, when she said without preamble or delay, "Mr. Hamilton, Red Stevens just died."

When you get to be an octogenarian, you grow as accustomed as one can to losing friends and family. But some of the losses hit you harder than others. This one shook me to my core. Amid all of the emotions and memories that flooded over me, I realized that I would have to do what Red would expect of me, which was simply to do my job.

I shifted into my lawyer mode and told Miss Hastings, "We will need to contact all of the family members, the various corporate boards and business interests, and be ready to control the media circus that will begin any minute."

Miss Hastings stood up and said, "I'll handle everything." She quickly walked to the door and then hesitated a moment. After an uncomfortable pause, during which I realized Margaret Hastings and I were crossing that line that divides professional and personal, she said quietly, "Mr. Hamilton, I am sorry for your loss."

Miss Hastings closed the door and left me alone with my thoughts.

———————

Two weeks later, I found myself at the head of our massive conference table with all of Red Stevens' various relatives gathered around. The feeling of anticipation—bordering on greed—was almost a physical presence in the room.

Knowing Red's feelings toward the majority of his relatives, I knew he would want me to prolong their misery as long as possible. Therefore, I had Margaret offer everyone coffee, tea, or soft drinks along with anything else she could think of. I scanned and rescanned the voluminous documents before me and cleared my throat multiple times. Finally, realizing that I was stretching the bounds of propriety, I rose to my feet and addressed the motley assemblage.

"Ladies and gentlemen, as you know, we are here to read the last will and testament of Howard 'Red' Stevens. I realize that this is a difficult time for all of us and that our personal losses individually far outweigh any legal or financial concerns we might have this morning."

I knew that wherever he was, Red would enjoy the irony.

"I will dispense with the preliminaries, the boilerplate, and the legalese, and will go directly to the issues at hand. Red Stevens was a very successful man in every sense of that word. His bequests are much as Red was himself—very simple and straightforward.

"I drew up this revised will for Mr. Stevens just over a year ago on his seventy-fifth birthday. I know from our subsequent conversations that this document does, indeed, reflect his final wishes. I will read directly from his will, and you will realize as I read that while this document is totally legal and binding, some of the passages are in Red's own words.

"To my eldest son, Jack Stevens, I leave my first company, Panhandle Oil and Gas. At the writing of this will, Panhandle's worth is somewhere in the neighborhood of $600 million."

Several gasps could be heard from around the table along with one prolonged, audible squeal of glee. I set the document down on the edge of the table and looked over the top of my reading glasses with my most intimidating courtroom stare. After a significant pause, I picked up the will and continued.

"Although Jack will be the sole owner of the company, its management and operations will be left in the hands of Panhandle's board of directors, which has served me so well over so many years. Jack, I want you to know that since you didn't have any interest in the company when I was living, I figured you wouldn't have any interest now that I'm gone. And letting you control something like Panhandle would be like giving a three-year-old a loaded gun. I want you to know that I have instructed Mr. Hamilton to write this will in such a way that if you fight for control or hinder the board or even complain about the nature of my bequest to you, the entire ownership of Panhandle Oil and Gas will immediately go to charity."

I looked up from the will and stared at Jack Stevens. The entire range of possible emotions was displayed on his face. Jack Stevens was a fifty-seven-year-old playboy who had never known the privilege of earning a day's wages. He had no idea of the favor his father had done for him by taking the control of Panhandle Oil and Gas out of his hands. I knew he was feeling that this was just one more time when he failed to live up to his illustrious father's expectations.

I actually felt some pity for Jack as I explained, "Mr. Stevens, the will does direct that each bequest be read in order and that the parties be dismissed after the portion of the document pertaining to them has been read."

He looked at me with a confused expression on his countenance and said, "What?"

At that point, always vigilant Miss Hastings took his arm and said, "Mr. Stevens, I'll escort you to the door."

When everyone had settled back into their chairs, and the level of anticipation had again risen to a fever pitch, I continued.

"To my only daughter, Ruth, I leave the family home and ranch in Austin, Texas, along with all working cattle operations."

Ruth was seated at the far end of the table with her dubious husband and offspring. Even at that distance, the sound of her hands slapping together and greedily rubbing back and forth could be heard. She and her family were so self-absorbed that I do not believe they understood the fact that the entire operation would be managed for them and that they would be kept at arm's length where they could not hurt themselves or anyone else. Miss Hastings promptly showed them from the room.

I cleared my throat and continued. "To my youngest son, and only other remaining child, Bill, I leave the entire holdings of my stock, bond, and investment portfolio. However, Bill, this portfolio will be left in the hands of Mr. Hamilton and his firm to be managed in trust for you and your heirs so that there will be something left to divide when somebody is reading your will someday."

The room continued to clear as each of the more distant relatives received their eagerly awaited windfall. Finally, there was but one, lone occupant of the room remaining with Miss Hastings and me.

I looked down the table at young Jason Stevens, the twenty-four-year-old great-nephew of my longtime friend, Red Stevens. He glared back at me with a look of rage, defiance, and disrespect that only someone who has made a lifelong practice of selfish anger can muster.

He slammed his hand on the table and yelled at me, "I knew that mean old man wouldn't leave anything for me. He always hated me." He stood and began to stomp out of the room.

"Not so fast," I called to him. "You are, indeed, mentioned here in the will."

He slid back into his chair and stared toward me, stone-faced, not wanting to signal the hope he felt.

I returned his cold stare, determined not to speak until he did. Patience comes easily to those of us who have seen eighty birthdays. Finally, when he could stand it no longer, he said, "Okay, what did the old goat give me?"

As I sat down and reached for the document, I heard young Jason Stevens mutter, "I bet it's nothing."

I sat back in my chair and smiled at him as I said, "Young man, it is, indeed, nothing and everything—both at the same time."

TWO

A Voice from the Past

In the end, a person is only known

by the impact he or she has on others.

J ason Stevens and I sat in silence as Miss Hastings left the room and quickly returned with a large cardboard box. She set the box next to me at the end of the table and took her customary place on my right.

I turned to Jason and said, "Young man, this box was given to me by your great-uncle, Red Stevens, on the day he prepared his last will and testament. The box was sealed at that time and has been kept in our vault per Mr. Stevens' instructions until today. As you can plainly see, the seal is still intact. There are very specific and detailed instructions as to how I am to administer this gift to you."

I broke open the seal, reached inside the box, and took out a videotape. I handed it to Miss Hastings, and she put the tape in the video player contained in the built-in console at the end of the conference room. She sat down next to me holding the remote control.

Jason Stevens blurted out, "What's going on here? Everyone else walks out with millions of dollars, and I get some kind of home movie."

I tried to ignore his smug attitude and replied, "I think it will all become clear to you shortly."

I nodded to Miss Hastings. She dimmed the lights and started the video. After some brief static, the image of seventy-five-year-old Red Stevens appeared on the screen. Red Stevens was a big man in every sense of that word. He had come to Texas out of the swamps of Louisiana with nothing but determination, strength, and the clothes on his back, and during the Depression and war years, had built an oil and cattle empire that rivaled any in the world. He was the kind of man who dominated every situation in which he was involved. Even now, with just his video image on the large screen at the end of the conference room, I could feel the energy level in the room climbing.

Red Stevens cleared his throat and began to speak. "Well, Jason, since you're watching this videotape, we will assume that I have kicked the bucket, bit the dust, bought the farm, and gone on to my just rewards. I know that my instructions have been followed to the letter, so you are viewing this video with my oldest and dearest friend, Theodore Hamilton, and his trusted associate, Margaret Hastings. Son, you don't know enough to realize it, but these are two of the finest people to ever walk God's green earth."

Red paused for a minute and then spoke directly to Margaret and me using a derivative of my name that only Red Stevens was allowed to use.

"Ted, I want to thank both you and Margaret for dealing with all of my in-laws, outlaws, and assorted misfit relatives earlier today. I know that none of them will win any prizes. I also want to apologize to both of you for the sorry attitude that I'm sure Jason has already displayed during these proceedings."

Red paused for another brief moment, cleared his throat, and began again. "Jason, I lived my life in a big way. I had a lot of big accomplishments, and I made a lot of big mistakes. One of the biggest mistakes I ever made was when I gave everyone in our family everything that they thought they ever wanted. It took me many years to figure out that everything we ever do or know or have in this life is a gift from the good Lord. He has a special plan for each of us, and He has provided everything we need to fulfill that plan. I spent many years trying to achieve happiness or buy it for friends and family. Only as an old man did I come to learn that all happiness comes from the gifts that God has given us. Unfortunately, the money and possessions I spread around didn't help people to understand the gifts that have been provided for us. In trying to make up for all the times I wasn't there, I gave them all material things. In doing so, I robbed them of everything that makes life wonderful.

"Gratefully, I also discovered God is merciful, and I believe I've made peace within regarding my shortcomings. However, I think my family members are all permanently ruined. It's like when a horse goes bad. You simply have to take him out and shoot him. Unfortunately, as my lawyer Mr. Hamilton advised me, shooting our entire family would be frowned upon. He also rightly reminded me that God never gives up on people. Therefore, I leave my family in God's hands, and I have taken steps in my will to provide a living for all of these relatives even if they will never experience life.

"You, on the other hand, Jason, may be the last great vestige of hope in our family. Although your life to date seems to be a sorry excuse for anything I would call promising, there does seem to be some spark of something in you I am hoping we can capture and fan into a flame. For that reason, I am not making you an instant millionaire for the rest of your life."

Jason slammed his open palm onto the conference table and began to speak, but was interrupted by Red Stevens' words from the videotape. "Now, Jason, before you mouth off and embarrass both you and me in front of these fine people, let me explain the ground rules here.

"On the first of each month for the next year, you will meet with Mr. Hamilton and Miss Hastings and be given one element of what I call the ultimate gift.

"If you stay the course over the next year, and embrace each element, at that point you will be the recipient of the most significant bequest I can leave you through my will. But understand, if at any time you do not perform as indicated, or if you give Mr. Hamilton or Miss Hastings an undue amount of difficulty, I have instructed Mr. Hamilton, through my will, to stop the process and leave you with nothing."

I heard a deep sigh and exhalation of breath from the direction of Jason Stevens.

Red continued. "Now, don't forget, boy. If you turn out to be more trouble than you're worth—which is not difficult for you— Mr. Hamilton will simply cut you off without another word.

"And, finally, to you, Theodore J. Hamilton," Red chuckled and continued. "I bet you didn't think I remembered your real name, Ted. I want to thank you for undertaking this little salvage operation on my behalf with Jason. And I also want to thank you for being the best friend that any man ever had. I accumulated a lot of things in my life, but I would trade them all in an instant for the privilege I have of sitting here, right now, and being able to say that Theodore J. Hamilton was my friend."

At that point, the video ended, and we all sat in silence. Finally, Jason turned to me and, in a belligerent tone, said, "That old man was crazy."

I sighed and replied, "Well, young man, it is certain that someone is crazy, and I think this little project is going to give us all the opportunity to find out who that someone may be."

I stood and offered my hand to Jason as I moved toward the door. He ignored my outstretched hand and said, "Wait a minute. What's the deal here? Why don't you just tell me what's going on, and what I get?"

"All in good time, young man," I said to him over my shoulder as I walked out of the room.

I could hear Jason's angry voice as I retreated down the hall. "Why couldn't he just leave me money like everybody else?"

I could hear the calm voice of Miss Hastings reply, "He loved you too much to do that."

THREE

THE GIFT OF WORK

He who loves his work never labors.

I must say I was rather anxious during the ensuing weeks and very relieved when the first day of the next month rolled around. I was sitting in my office working on other matters trying to keep my mind occupied and off of the fact that Jason Stevens would be arriving shortly.

Finally, the buzzer on my telephone sounded, and Miss Hastings informed me that young Jason Stevens had arrived and was waiting in the conference room. I collected the appropriate files while Miss Hastings retrieved Red Stevens' box from the vault. When we entered the conference room, we found Jason slumped back in a chair with his feet up on the conference table. I strode across the room and slid the box that Margaret had handed me onto the table in such a way as to knock Jason's feet off of it.

"Good morning, Jason," I said. "I'm glad that you found a chair and are making yourself comfortable. Some people never have learned the proper use of furniture."

Jason dismissed my comment with a bored wave and replied, "Can we just get on with it here? I've got things to do and people to see."

I laughed aloud as I sat down and said, "Young man, I do anticipate you will have things to do and people to see, but it may not be exactly as you think."

I took another videotape from the box and handed it to Margaret. She placed it in the video player and, in a few moments, Red Stevens appeared on the large screen. He said, "Good morning, Ted, and to you, Miss Hastings. Once again, I want to thank you for undertaking this little chore. And, Jason, I want to remind you of the rules. If at any time during the next twelve months you do not perform as called for, or if Mr. Hamilton does not approve of your attitude and demeanor, he will simply stop the process and cut you off from my ultimate gift to you.

"I will warn you about Mr. Hamilton. He may appear very patient and long-suffering, but, young man, if you push him too far, you will find that you have let an angry tiger out of its cage."

Jason looked at me with a bewildered expression on his face. I simply stared back at him.

Red paused and seemed to be remembering days gone by. "Jason, when I was much younger than you are now," he continued, "I learned the satisfaction that comes from a simple four-letter word: work. One of the things my wealth has robbed from you and the entire family is the privilege and satisfaction that comes from doing an honest day's work."

I could see Jason rolling his eyes as he let out a deep sigh.

"Now, before you go off the deep end and reject everything I'm going to tell you," Red continued, "I want you to realize that work has brought me everything I have and everything that you have. I regret that I have taken from you the joy of knowing that what you have is what you've earned.

"My earliest memories in the swamps of Louisiana are of work—hard, backbreaking labor that as a young man I resented greatly. My parents had too many mouths to feed and not enough food, so if we wanted to eat, we worked. Later, when I was on my own and came to Texas, I realized that hard work had become a habit for me, and it has served as a true joy all the rest of my life.

"Jason, you have enjoyed the best things that this world has to offer. You have been everywhere, seen everything, and done everything. What you don't understand is how much pleasure these things can bring you when you have earned them yourself, when leisure becomes a reward for hard work instead of a way to avoid work.

"Tomorrow morning, you are going to take a little trip with Mr. Hamilton and Miss Hastings. You will be going to meet an old friend of mine on a ranch outside of Alpine, Texas. When I was young and struggling to stay alive during the Depression, I met Gus Caldwell. We learned the power of hard work then, and today there's no one better to teach you this lesson than Gus.

"I have already prepared a letter outlining this entire situation to be sent to Gus Caldwell. Mr. Hamilton has forwarded that letter to Alpine, Texas, and Gus Caldwell will be expecting you.

"Please remember, if at any time you do not complete the activities outlined in my will, or if Mr. Hamilton is not pleased with your attitude, this endeavor will simply end, and you will forego the ultimate gift."

The screen went black.

"This is ridiculous," Jason shot at me angrily.

I smiled and replied, "Yes, dealing with you can be trying, but there are some things you just do for friends like Red Stevens. I will see you at the airport at 6:45 in the morning."

Jason looked at me as if he were addressing an imbecile. "Didn't they have any flights later in the day?" he asked.

I replied with more patience than I felt, "Yes, but Mr. Caldwell—I think you will find—is not one who wants to waste any time. See you tomorrow."

Jason left our office, and Miss Hastings made all of the necessary arrangements.

The next morning, just as the airline attendant was preparing to close the door, a bleary-eyed Jason Stevens came running down the concourse. Miss Hastings handed the attendant the tickets for the three of us, and we boarded the plane.

Miss Hastings and I took our assigned seats, which were the first two on the right side of the aircraft in the first-class section. Jason stood there with a confused expression on his face as there were no more seats in the first-class cabin.

He turned to me and asked, "Where's my seat?"

Miss Hastings responded to his question using her most efficient tone, but I knew she was enjoying every moment of it when she said, "Oh, Mr. Stevens, you have been assigned seat 23F."

She handed Jason his ticket stub, and he stomped down the aisle toward the coach seating.

When we got off the plane at the Midland-Odessa airport, Gus Caldwell was there to meet us. I had known Gus for years as a friend and associate of Red Stevens. We shared a mutual love of our lifetime friend. Gus shook my hand warmly with the callused grip of a man of thirty-five instead of what I knew must be his real age of seventy-five. He greeted Miss Hastings politely but was somewhat gruff with Jason.

He said to him, "Red Stevens was one of the best men I ever met. I don't see how you're going to live up to that."

As Jason was preparing to protest this cold greeting, Gus shot back at him, "Son, why don't you go downstairs and see if you can find the luggage. Make yourself useful."

A few moments later, we were downstairs in the airport, and Jason had, indeed, located all of the luggage. Gus pulled around the parking lot to pick us up at the door in his deluxe pickup truck—a vehicle we rarely see in Boston. Gus held the door for Miss Hastings and me and said to Jason, "Well, don't just stand there, boy. Get these bags in the truck."

Jason loaded all of the luggage in the bed of the pickup truck and then asked sheepishly, "Where am I supposed to sit?"

"You can ride in the back or walk," Gus said. "It's all the same to me."

Gus got in and began to pull away just as Jason scrambled into the bed of the pickup truck. I glanced back and saw him sprawled out among the luggage, rolling from side to side, as Gus summarily ignored all of the speed limit signs as we left the airport complex.

During the ride out to Gus' sprawling ranch, with Jason out of earshot, we discussed memories of Red and our desire to help Red redeem Jason Stevens. We agreed that Gus would spend the next four weeks communicating his version of the work ethic to Jason while Miss Hastings and I would leave the following day and spend several weeks in Austin, where I was to do some legislative work for another client.

After traversing what seemed to be an endless gravel road, we turned into a driveway that led off into the distance. A sign read: Gus Caldwell Ranch. Friends are welcome. Trespassers will be shot.

After another ten-minute drive, we arrived at a huge ranch house where we were greeted by Gus' extended family, several of his workers, and a number of dogs. Gus led Miss Hastings and me into his comfortable home and yelled back at Jason, "Don't just lie there in the truck, boy. Get the bags."

Gus had informed Miss Hastings and me that the next day would start early at the Caldwell ranch. He decided to let Jason find out the hard way.

The next morning, Miss Hastings and I, and all of the Caldwell family, enjoyed a huge breakfast of monumental cholesterol before 6:00 a.m. As we were enjoying our second cups of coffee, Gus said, "Well, I better go get Sleeping Beauty. This is going to be an interesting day. Real educational, if you know what I mean."

We could hear Gus climbing the stairs and banging open the door to Jason's room. He called out in a thunderous voice, "Boy, are you alive? You're sleeping through the whole day, here. Get dressed and get downstairs."

Gus rejoined us as we chatted amiably over the strong coffee, and a few minutes later, a disheveled, sleepy-eyed Jason joined us. He sat down at the table. No sooner was he seated than Gus rose and said, "Well, that was a good breakfast. Time to get to work."

Jason glared at him and said belligerently, "Can I have some breakfast, please?"

Gus smiled and said, "Yes, sir. First thing tomorrow morning. Nobody ever leaves Gus Caldwell's home hungry. But there's not much I can do if people are going to sleep all day."

Jason looked out the window and exclaimed, "It's not even daylight yet."

Gus chuckled and replied, "That's very observant, son. I thought I was going to have to teach you everything. Now get out to the bunkhouse and see if you can find some work clothes. That's about the most worthless get-up you have on there I've ever seen. We'll be leaving in about five minutes."

Gus agreed to take Miss Hastings and me out to where Jason would be working to see him get started before we left for Austin. We were seated in the truck when Jason stumbled out of the bunkhouse and dutifully climbed into the back of the pickup truck. Before he was seated, Gus shot out across the yard and drove through a gate, bouncing out across an immense field.

Just as the sun was rising, Gus stopped at a remote corner of the ranch where a huge pile of fence posts lay on the ground. Gus jumped out of the truck and yelled, "Boy, would you get out of that pickup bed. I've never seen one for lyin' around like you."

Miss Hastings and I followed Gus and Jason to the last fence post standing in a long line that stretched out of sight. "Welcome to Fence Post 101," Gus proclaimed proudly. He quickly showed Jason how to dig a post hole, set the post, and string the wire in a straight line. Even at seventy-five, Gus Caldwell showed immense strength and incredible stamina. He made everything look easy.

He turned to Jason and said, "Now, you try." And Gus joined Miss Hastings and me near the truck.

Jason stumbled through the process almost comically, and Gus called out, "Well, hopefully you'll get the hang of it before you beat yourself to death. Somebody will come by to pick you up for the noon meal."

Jason seemed alarmed and called out, "How far is this fence supposed to go?"

As Gus helped Miss Hastings and me into the truck, Gus laughed and said, "No more than a mile, and then we'll turn and go the other way. Don't worry. We won't run out of things for you to do. I wish I had a dollar for every post hole good old Red Stevens and I dug all across Texas."

We left Jason there to his labors.

Almost four weeks later, Miss Hastings and I returned from a successful trip to the Texas state capitol in Austin. Gus, once again, picked us up at the airport, and as we were driving to his ranch, I couldn't help but ask, "Well, how is young Jason getting along?"

Gus chuckled and said, "I wasn't sure he was going to make it. Between the sunburn, blisters, and heat exhaustion, it was a close thing, but I think you are in for a pleasant surprise."

When we reached the ranch, Gus drove us directly to the field where Jason had been working the first day. I noticed that the fence extended far beyond its original point, and Jason was nowhere in sight. Gus drove on a distance, and once we crested a short rise, I spotted Jason in the distance.

An amazing transformation had taken place. Jason was browned by the sun, lean from his physical labor, and working steadily as we arrived. He waved to us and walked over to join us as we got out of the truck.

"Jason, did you dig all of those post holes and set all of those posts yourself?" I asked.

He seemed to have a gleam in his eye as he answered, "Yes, sir. Every one of them. And they're straight, too."

Gus put his arm around Jason's shoulder and said, "Son, I wasn't sure you were going to make it, but you turned into a really good hand. Your great-uncle, Red, and I discovered nearly sixty years ago that if you can do this kind of work with pride and quality, then you can do anything. I think you've learned your lesson. Now it's time to get you back to Boston."

I was shocked when Jason replied, "I only have a few more to finish up this section. Why don't we leave in the morning?"

———

The next day, after breakfast, Gus volunteered to drive us to the airport. Jason dutifully carried the bags out onto the porch, but instead of the pickup truck, Gus was driving a new Cadillac.

Jason laughed and asked, "Where's your truck, Mr. Caldwell?"

Gus smiled and replied, "I can't have one of my best hands

rolling around in the back of the truck with the luggage. Now let's get you to the airport."

———————

As we flew 30,000 feet above middle America, I couldn't help but think of Red Stevens and the lesson on work he had taught Jason. I hoped the lesson meant as much to Jason as it did to me.

Money is nothing more than a tool.
It can be a force for good,
a force for evil, or simply be idle.

FOUR

The Gift of Money

There are certain times in this life that you find yourself pursuing a course that you are not certain will prove to be fruitful. Then, all of a sudden, out of nowhere, miraculously you receive the smallest sign or indication that you're on the right track. Just such a moment occurred when Jason Stevens came in for our second monthly meeting.

Jason and I were seated in our customary spots in the conference room discussing his work experience in Alpine, Texas. Miss Hastings returned from the vault carrying Red Stevens' box. With no prompting or forewarning, Jason got out of his chair and helped Miss Hastings by taking the box from her and carrying it to the end of the table.

To most people, this, in and of itself, would seem like nothing—or at most an extremely small thing. However, I recognized how Jason had been raised and that he had always taken such minor courtesies for granted. I chose to look upon this incident, even if small, as a positive sign.

Red Stevens stared back at us from the large screen. He had a bit of a mischievous grin on his face which I suspect came from his private thoughts about Jason's work experience on Gus Caldwell's ranch.

His voice boomed out, "Well, Jason, welcome back from the Garden of Eden—better known as Texas. Since I am talking to you now, I will assume you survived a month with Gus Caldwell. I always found that soaking blistered hands helped."

I actually heard Jason let out what might be described as a brief chuckle.

Red continued. "Today, we are going to talk about what may, indeed, be the most misunderstood commodity in the world. That is, money. There is absolutely nothing that can replace money in the things that money does, but regarding the rest of the things in the world, money is absolutely useless.

"For example, all the money in the world won't buy you one more day of life. That's why you're watching this videotape right now. And it's important to realize that money will not make you happy. I hasten to add that poverty will not make you happy either. I have been rich, and I have been poor—and all other things being equal—rich is better."

At that, we all laughed.

Red took on a more serious expression and continued. "Jason, you have no idea or concept of the value of money. That is not your fault. That is my fault. But I am hoping in the next thirty days, you can begin to understand what money means in the lives of real people in the real world. More of the violence, anxiety, divorce, and mistrust in the world is caused by misunderstanding money than any other factor. These are concepts that are foreign to you because money to you has always seemed like the air you breathe. There's always more. All you have to do is take the next breath.

"I know that you have always flashed around a lot of money and spent it frivolously. I take the responsibility for this situation because I deprived you of the privilege of understanding the fair exchange between work and money.

"Last month, you began to get just an inkling of the pride and satisfaction that can come from doing a good job even at the most menial task. Since money is the result of most people's labor, I think you need to begin to understand it.

"If Gus Caldwell had paid you for the work you performed last month, you would have earned approximately $1,500. I know that it seems like almost nothing to you, but I can assure you it is the going rate.

"When you leave today, Mr. Hamilton will hand you an envelope that is inside the box. The envelope contains $1,500. During the next month, I want you to go out and find five different people who are in situations where a portion of that $1,500 can make a real difference in their lives. I want you to notice how anxiety caused by a lack of money is affecting them in real ways, and how once you give them the money, they can focus on real and important issues in their world.

"I realize that in the past you have probably blown $1,500 in a few hours with some of your so-called friends. Now it's time to begin understanding what $1,500 can do if it's put in the right place.

"By the end of this month, you will report five such instances to Mr. Hamilton, describing each situation and what you did about it. If Mr. Hamilton feels you have learned the lesson of the gift of money, I will talk with you next month."

Red's image faded from the video screen, and we sat in silence for a few moments.

Jason turned to me and said, "I'm not sure I understand what it is I'm supposed to do. Where do I find these people, and how much—"

I interrupted him by explaining, "Young man, you heard your instructions just as I did. I am not authorized to give you any additional information or assistance. This lesson, like all of the others your great-uncle is trying to teach you, is one you must learn primarily yourself. I can assure you that Red Stevens was a thorough man, and he has given you everything you need to succeed."

I reached into the box and took out a small envelope just as Red had described. I handed the envelope to Jason and said, "We will look forward to hearing from you on or before the end of the month."

Jason rose slowly with a bewildered expression on his face. He turned and slowly retreated to the door. Miss Hastings and I remained in the conference room for several minutes. Finally, she broke the silence. "I don't think he has any concept of what to do with that envelope full of money."

I thought for a moment and then replied, "Most of us have learned about money over a number of years. Jason has been absent from school, and he has a lot of catching up to do."

———

It was the next to the last day of the month before we heard from Jason, and I will admit to being a bit anxious about his progress. Jason arranged an appointment for the next morning. At the appointed hour, Miss Hastings ushered him into my office, and he and Miss Hastings sat in the two leather chairs in front of my desk.

Jason seemed a bit nervous and uncertain of himself. I paused for a few moments, thinking about what I might have done had I been given one month to find five people whose lives I could affect with money. I resigned myself to performing my tasks as Red Stevens' attorney and the executor of his estate. I knew that if Jason had not lived up to the letter of the agreement, I would have to end the journey at that point. That was a prospect that did not appeal to me for Jason's sake and, I must admit, for my own as well.

Finally, I turned to Jason and asked, "Well, young man, are you prepared to present your report?"

Jason nodded and drew a piece of crumpled paper from his inside jacket pocket. He cleared his throat and began to speak slowly. "Well, I'm not quite sure if this is right, but here goes.

"First, I was driving late one evening and passed one of those fund-raising car washes people hold in parking lots. It was nearly dark, so I knew they were about done for the day. I asked the man in charge what group this was and how they were doing. He told me that it was a group of inner-city Boy Scouts who were trying to raise the money to go to their Jamboree the following week. He went on to explain that it had been a bit disappointing because this was their last effort, and since they were a bit short, at least one or two of the boys were not going to be able to go. I asked him how much they needed to reach their goal. He seemed discouraged when he replied that they were almost $200 short, and they were going to have to clear the lot within ten minutes. I pulled my car into the space designated and told the boys to do their best job. When they were done, I handed one of the boys $200 and drove away."

Jason looked up at me seeking approval. I merely nodded for him to continue. Although he was still shaky, he seemed to be gaining momentum as he consulted his sheet.

"Next, I found myself at the mall looking for a parking space. I spotted a young woman holding a baby, standing in front of an old car, and shouting at a guy driving a tow truck parked behind her. The two seemed to be really arguing, and since they had one of the best parking spaces, I stopped and asked what the trouble was. The guy told me he worked for ABC Used Cars and that the girl had missed her last two payments. He told me that the payments were only $100 a month on an old junker like that. The girl began crying and said that her baby had been sick, and if she lost her car, she wouldn't be able to keep her job, and then she didn't know what would happen. I asked the tow truck driver how much the balance was on her car loan. He told me it was four more payments of $100 each. I gave him $400 and got a paid-in-full receipt for the young mother. Here's a copy."

Jason dropped a soiled and creased receipt on the edge of my desk, and then he pressed on. "While I was in the mall, I discovered a young husband and wife with two small children shopping in a toy store. Each of the children repeatedly asked for various toys, but their parents regrettably told them that Santa Claus probably wouldn't come this year since their father had lost his job. While the children were at the end of another aisle looking at some stuffed animals, I handed the mother $300 and asked her to be sure that Santa made it to their house this year.

"As I was leaving the mall, I noticed an old woman sitting on a bench. As I passed, she dropped her purse, and when I picked it up to hand it back to her, I noticed that she had been crying. When I asked her what the problem was, she told me that her husband, Harold, and she had been married fifty-seven years and, for the first time in their lives, they just couldn't make it. His heart pills cost over $60 a month, and the pharmacy in the mall wouldn't take her food stamps for the medicine. I spent $200 buying a three-month supply of Harold's heart medication and leaving her $20 to take him out for his favorite lunch."

Jason looked at me expectantly, and I smiled at him and said, "It sounds good so far, but you were instructed to find five examples."

Jason appeared more nervous than ever as he explained, "While driving one day, I discovered a car broken down at the side of the road. I got out and met a young man named Brian. He's about my age, and we found we have a lot in common. I used my cell phone to call a tow truck, and they towed him into a garage. The mechanic said the engine in the car was really shot and needed to be replaced.

"Brian was totally panicked because he needed the car to get back and forth to school and work. The mechanic said it would cost $700. Brian nearly went into shock because he didn't have any money, so I gave him the $700 he needed to get a new engine."

Ever efficient Miss Hastings seemed to have an emotional

quiver in her voice as she said, "Sir, that seems to add up to $1,800. I believe the original document called for only $1,500."

Jason seemed alarmed as he leaned forward in his chair and said, "Well, I put in $300 of my own money. Is that okay?"

Miss Hastings beat me to the punch and replied, "Of course, it's okay. Mr. Hamilton is a fair and reasonable man."

She glared at me and said, "Aren't you, Mr. Hamilton?"

I assured both Jason and the indomitable Miss Hastings that I was fair and reasonable, and Jason had learned an important lesson in the value of money. I hoped he would never forget his lesson. I knew I never would.

FIVE

THE GIFT OF FRIENDS

It is a wealthy person, indeed,
  who calculates riches
  not in gold but in friends.

T he next morning, Miss Hastings let me know that Jason Stevens had arrived and would be waiting in the conference room. After his successful journey into the realm of work and money, I had hoped that his sullen attitude would have improved; however, upon entering the conference room, I rapidly discovered this was not the case. Before I could even sit down, he started in on me.

"Look. Why do I have to go through all this stuff? This is ridiculous. You have a copy of the will. You must know what it is that I'm going to inherit. Why don't we just cut through all the garbage and get down to the bottom line?"

I smiled at him and said, "Good morning, Jason. It's nice to see you, too. I had hoped after your great-uncle's lesson in money, you would be more understanding of this process."

I rose to my feet slowly—which is not unusual when you're eighty years old. I gave him a stare that I had used successfully during my years as a judge. "Young man," I said, "you have two—and only two—options. You can go through this process the way Red Stevens laid it out for you, or you can quit right now; but I will tell you one thing, your attitude is putting you dangerously close to losing the ultimate gift that your great-uncle planned for you."

Jason leaned back in his chair and sighed. "Okay, let's get on with it," he said. "What's next?"

Miss Hastings brought in the box and set it on the table next to me. I took out the next videotape, and Miss Hastings started the VCR. Once again Red Stevens appeared and began to speak.

"Jason, as you heard me tell Mr. Hamilton at your first meeting, he is quite simply my best friend. *Friend* is a word that is thrown around far too easily by people who don't know the meaning of it. Today, people call everyone they know their friend. Young man, you're lucky if you live as long as I have and can count your real friends on the fingers of both hands.

"I am now going to share a story with you, Jason, that I promised I would never tell as long as I lived. Since you are watching this after my death, and in the presence of the one whom I promised, I feel comfortable sharing it. As you know, I lived past my seventy-fifth birthday and enjoyed what to most people was a long and healthy life. But this was not always a sure thing.

"I remember when I had just turned thirty-eight years old and was hospitalized with an extreme fever. The doctors weren't sure what was wrong with me, so they brought in every specialist from across the country. Finally, I was diagnosed as having a rare kidney disease which was incurable. The only hope they gave me was a new procedure called a kidney transplant.

"You've got to realize that this was unheard of at that time, and donors were not readily available as they are today. I called Mr. Hamilton, who has always acted as my attorney, and told him we would need to start a nationwide search to find me a kidney. I was very frightened because the specialist had told me that without the transplant I might not have more than a few weeks. You can imagine my relief when Mr. Hamilton called me two days later and told me he had located a kidney on the East Coast.

"Well, as I'm sure you can guess, the operation was a success and gave me back over half of my adult life. What I'm sure you couldn't guess, and what no one has known until now, is that the kidney that Mr. Hamilton found was his own."

Red paused on the videotape to take a drink of water, and young Jason Stevens stared at me in disbelief. On the big screen, Red continued. "There's only one way in the world to explain something like that, and it's called friendship. Now, Jason, I know you think you have a lot of friends. But the reality is, you have a lot of people who simply want your money or the things it will buy. Except for your time with Gus Caldwell, you've never worked a day in your life nor done anything I would call productive. But you have been the life of the party and an easy touch for a lot of weak hangers-on you casually call friends.

"During the next thirty days, I want you to spend a lot of time thinking and observing. I want you to find what you feel to be the principles that underlie true friendship, and I want you to be able to report to Mr. Hamilton an example of true friendship that demonstrates your principles. Jason, you will never do anything in your life that will bring more quality to your existence than growing to understand and nurture friendship."

The videotape ended, and Jason seemed to be deep in thought. Finally, he blurted out, "I don't understand. I mean—"

I interrupted him. "I know you don't understand. That's the whole point. I only hope that you will remember your great-uncle's words and, for your sake, by the end of the month you are at least beginning to understand. I will look forward to your report."

I walked out of the conference room, leaving young Jason Stevens to his assignment.

——◆——

On the last day of the month, Miss Hastings called into my office to let me know that Jason had set up an appointment and would be arriving within the hour. I sat back and thought about my lifelong friend, Red Stevens. I wasn't sure how you could teach someone the depth to which a friendship could grow, especially if the person had never experienced it himself. I will admit to feeling a great sense of doubt and foreboding as I considered Jason's prospects of succeeding in the task Red Stevens had given him.

As we gathered around the conference table, Miss Hastings and I were quiet. Both of us were observing Jason's expression and manner. He seemed to have a lot on his mind. He gave us each a perfunctory greeting and muttered, "I hope that ... well, I mean ... I just don't—"

Miss Hastings stopped him by saying, "I believe our agenda today involved your report to Mr. Hamilton on your progress with respect to understanding friendship."

Jason looked at me doubtfully, and I nodded and gave him a brief smile of encouragement.

He began. "I thought a lot about friendship this month, and I tried to come up with the principles that define friendship. The best I can do is to say that friendship involves loyalty, commitment, and a process that includes sharing another person's life.

It even goes deeper than that, but it's hard to put into words.

"The best example of friendship I can give to demonstrate my principles is a story that Gus Caldwell told me when I was working for him in Texas. He explained that when he and Uncle Red got started in the cattle business, they had ranches several miles apart, but they and several other ranchers all shared the same range. Each spring, all the ranchers would have what they call a roundup, which apparently involved collecting and branding all of the new calves, called yearlings, which had been born since the last roundup.

"As Mr. Caldwell explained it to me, the young calves simply follow their mothers wherever they go, so as the cattle are collected, representatives from each ranch are present to brand each new calf with the same brand as its mother's.

"Well, it seems that early on, Mr. Caldwell was very concerned that Uncle Red wasn't going to make it as a rancher. So, during the roundup one year, Gus simply branded a number of calves that should have been his own with Uncle Red's brand. He told me that he figured that he had been able to give over thirty calves to Uncle Red through that process.

"But at the end of the roundup, when Gus performed what is called a tally, which is simply counting all the cattle with his brand, he found that instead of being thirty calves short as he thought he should, he actually had almost fifty more than he started with.

"He was confused about that incident for many years until, while Mr. Caldwell and Uncle Red were on a fishing trip, Uncle Red told Gus that when they first got started, he had been worried about Gus making it in the business. Since he didn't want to lose his best friend and neighbor, he had actually branded a bunch of his calves with Gus Caldwell's brand."

Jason paused and glanced at both Miss Hastings and me for any sign of approval. He continued. "That story that Mr. Caldwell told me about my Uncle Red best describes how I understand each of the elements of friendship. I know it takes many years to build a friendship like that, but I think somehow it must be worth it.

"As you know, last month I met Brian when his car broke down at the side of the road. I helped him get a new engine for it, and since then we have done several things together, and I hope that someday we can be friends like Gus Caldwell and my Uncle Red."

Jason looked directly into my eyes and said, "And I hope I can be as good a friend as you were to Red Stevens."

I smiled at him and said, "In my best judgment, you have begun your lifetime lesson in friendship. The only thing I can tell you is that any effort you put into a friendship is always returned manyfold."

I thanked Jason for sharing the story about Red Stevens and Gus Caldwell. I had known for half a century that they were both great men and great friends. Jason's story, passed to him by Gus Caldwell, was just one more example of great friendship.

Miss Hastings walked Jason out of the conference room, leaving me alone with my memories.

As I sat back in my chair and remembered my lifelong friend, Red Stevens, I reflected that our friendship had begun simply and without either of us understanding what our relationship would grow to be. Jason had learned the beginnings of how to be a friend, and I hoped that his new friendship would blossom into a lifelong treasure giving him as much pleasure as Red Stevens and I had enjoyed.

SIX

THE GIFT OF LEARNING

Education is a lifelong journey
whose destination expands
as you travel.

Red Stevens' bequest to his great-nephew, Jason, represented the most unusual and, potentially, the most important matter I had ever handled for a client or a friend. As we entered the fourth month of our one-year journey with Jason, I wasn't sure how much progress we were making. He had shown many signs of improvement, but his belligerent, arrogant, and selfish attitude—borne of a life of idle privilege—still showed through from time to time.

As we began our monthly ritual around the conference room table, he interrupted the proceedings before Miss Hastings could even start the videotape.

"Look, I have done everything you have said up to this point, and this has all been well and good, but I need to have some idea of where we are going here and what I get at the end of all of this. I can't just waste a year out of my life."

I stared at Jason for several moments and tried to think of what Red would want me to say. Finally, I responded. "Jason, it seems to me that your entire life to date has been a series of wasted years. I don't see how this one-year acquiescence to your great-uncle's will could do anything but improve your track record; however, you do have the option to stop this process at any point in time."

He fired back at me, "Can't you just give me some idea of what I am going to get out of this so I can decide if it's all worth it?"

I gave him my courtroom stare and stated, "Young man, I am bound by honor, duty, and friendship to perform each step of this process as directed by Red Stevens. I have no option in the matter.

You, indeed, do have an option. Either you play or you don't play, but if you're going to play, you're going to play by the rules. Is there any part of that you don't understand?"

Jason and I locked eyes, and we were in a staring contest that represented a test of wills. Unfortunately for him, my will had been tested many, many times over eighty years, and his was only just now being tested due to the love and concern of Red Stevens.

He finally looked away and mumbled, "Okay, let's play the video."

Red Stevens appeared on the screen and seemed to display a bit more intensity than before. It seemed that as we cleared each hurdle, the one before us seemed to take on more importance and significance.

Red began. "Jason, the next element of the gift I am trying to leave to you encompasses knowledge and learning. As you know, I never had the benefit of a formal education, and I realize that you have some kind of degree from that high-toned college we sent you to that is little more than a playground for the idle rich."

Jason leaned back in his chair, slammed his fist onto the table, and blew out a long stream of air.

Red continued. "Now, before you get your feelings all hurt, I want you to realize that I respect universities as well as any type of formal education. It just wasn't a part of my life. What was a part of my life was a constant curiosity and desire to learn everything I could about the people and world around me. I wasn't able to go to school very long after I learned to read, but the ability to read, think, and observe made me a relatively well-educated man.

"But learning is a process. You can't simply sit in a classroom and someday walk offstage with a sheepskin and call yourself educated. I believe the reason a graduation ceremony is called a commencement is because the process of learning begins—or commences—at that point. The schooling that went before simply provided the tools and the framework for the real lessons to come.

"In the final analysis, Jason, life—when lived on your own terms—is the ultimate teacher. My wealth and success have robbed you of that, and this is my best effort to repair the damage."

Red paused for a few seconds, collected his thoughts, and continued. "Jason, you are going to be going on a little trip. Mr. Hamilton and Miss Hastings will be accompanying you. Your destination will be the greatest source of learning I ever discovered. If you will keep an open mind, you will find the key to the gift of learning that will serve you all the days of your life.

"After one month in this great place of learning, you must be able to explain to Mr. Hamilton—to his satisfaction—the fundamental key to all learning, education, and knowledge. Mr. Hamilton has all of the details and will give them to you as you need them. I wish you well."

Miss Hastings got up to retrieve the videotape as Jason asked in a bored but resigned tone, "Where do we have to go, and what do we have to do?"

As I stood and started walking out of the room, I said, "Jason, we don't have to go anywhere or do anything. We can stop this process right now, but if you want to continue, be at the airport, Gate 27, at seven in the morning. Bring your passport, some summer clothes, and a good attitude."

The next morning, we actually met Jason—luggage in hand—crossing the long-term parking lot outside of the airport. I called to him, "Jason—good morning. I'm surprised to see you here a half-hour before the plane leaves."

He laughed and said, "I thought I'd try to catch one without running a hundred-yard dash and squeezing in as they close the door."

Miss Hastings took my arm as we crossed the driveway toward the terminal. She whispered to me, "It may be small and slow, but it does seem to be progress, indeed."

Jason caught up with us and asked, "So, where are we going?"

I smiled at him and replied, "South America."

Jason stopped in his tracks and asked, "What university or graduate school is located in South America?"

Miss Hastings responded to his question cheerily, "I'm quite certain you have never heard of it."

Three flights later, we found ourselves in a rickety taxi, winding along a dirt road with dense jungle on either side. Eventually, we arrived at a dusty village with dirt streets and a few dilapidated buildings running along the edge of the jungle.

The taxi stopped in front of the largest building on the street, and we got out and retrieved our luggage. As the taxi drove off in a cloud of dust, Jason asked incredulously, "Are you sure we're in the right place?"

I laughed and replied, "Education and learning are where you find them."

We got settled into our three rooms in the modest but surprisingly comfortable hotel and agreed to meet in the lobby for breakfast the next day. I was very tired and fended off each of Jason's queries by simply telling him that the lesson would begin in the morning.

With the hectic day of travel behind me, I slept well and met Miss Hastings in the lobby, where she had already procured a table for us at the edge of what passed for a dining room. Several moments later, Jason arrived, and we ate a quick and simple breakfast.

As I got up from the table, I said, "Jason, we're going to walk down to the end of this street. There's a building there where your education will begin."

Jason stood and sighed, saying, "I've come this far. I may as well see what my crazy great-uncle had in mind."

As we walked along the dusty street, the three of us must have made quite a conspicuous sight, as many of the local residents came out to look at us. There were many simple wood and sheet-metal structures, and as we got to the end of the street, the last building on the left was slightly larger and more modern than the rest. A sign over the door in both Spanish and English read,

Howard "Red" Stevens Library.

When Jason spotted the name, he began to laugh and asked, "What is going on?"

As I climbed the three steps and opened the door, I said, "I think you'll find out what you need to know inside."

We entered the library and were greeted by a pleasant young woman at the counter. She spoke English very well as she greeted us and said, "I assume you are Mr. Hamilton and Miss Hastings."

I nodded yes, and her eyes brightened as she looked at Jason and exclaimed, "You must be Jason Stevens. We are very proud to have you here. Señor Red Stevens was a great man who helped all the people in our village."

I cleared my throat and said, "Jason, for the next four weeks, you will be assisting the librarian in her duties. You will have everything you need here to learn the lesson that your great-uncle wants you to learn."

Jason raised his voice louder than necessary and stated, "I may not have done well in school or learned much in college, but I can't believe that there is anything to be learned in this tiny place that I haven't had access to before."

Jason turned a complete circle as he surveyed the one-room library.

"This place is made up mostly of empty shelves. There's only a handful of books here," he observed.

The librarian smiled and explained, "All of the books are being read by people in our village and for miles around. Your great-uncle told us when he gave us this library that books don't do any good sitting on the shelf."

I told Jason that Miss Hastings and I would be leaving him to his work, but we would be checking in on him daily.

Over the next four weeks, I slipped into the pleasant lifestyle of the village. Miss Hastings and I took several side trips and had ample opportunities for sightseeing and the collection of native artwork. The people were all friendly and pleasant, especially as they learned that I represented their late, great benefactor Red Stevens.

As we checked on Jason each day, we discovered he was actually going about his task with more energy and diligence than I had expected. He became proficient at getting the books checked in and checked out rapidly, and he would often converse with the library patrons about the books that they had read.

As the last day of our scheduled trip arrived, I almost hated to leave the pleasant village. Everyone came onto the street to wish us well, and we departed in what seemed to be the same cab in which we had arrived.

After a hard day of traveling, we found ourselves back at the Boston airport, where we collected our luggage and walked toward the parking lot.

Jason hurried a few steps in front of us, turned to block our path, and said, "Hold it right here. I did everything that you said, I worked hard in the library, and I looked at every book they had in that dinky little place. There was nothing new to be learned there.

The only thing that I found out is that there are good and simple people who will get up hours before daylight and will walk many miles along mountain trails to get a tattered old copy of a book. The only thing I can honestly say I know now that I didn't know when we left here four weeks ago is that the desire and hunger for education is the key to real learning."

As Miss Hastings and I stepped around either side of Jason and moved toward the car, I called over my shoulder, "Congratulations, young man. I will see you in the office on Monday, and we will discover where we go from here."

Miss Hastings and I got our luggage into the trunk of the car, and as we drove through the exit of the airport parking lot, I could still see Jason rooted in the same place—no doubt thinking about the lesson we had all learned.

SEVEN

THE GIFT OF PROBLEMS

Problems can only be avoided
by exercising good judgment.
Good judgment can only be gained
by experiencing life's problems.

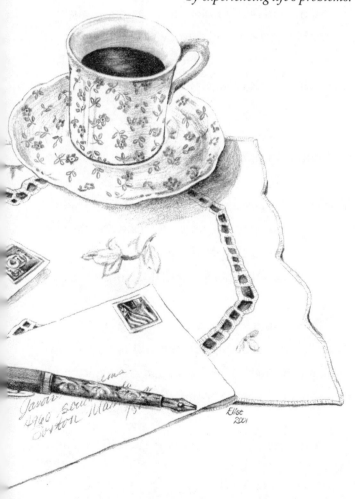

I will admit to having a sense of anticipation the following Monday as I contemplated the possible direction of the next act in Jason Stevens' life drama. I marveled at how my oldest and dearest friend, Red Stevens, could reach out from beyond the grave to impact a young life.

At the appointed hour, Miss Hastings ushered Jason into the conference room and summoned me to our monthly encounter with destiny. Jason seemed to be more mature and confident than he had been just four short months earlier. He actually greeted both Miss Hastings and me as we began the next phase of our odyssey.

The image of Red Stevens materialized onto the large screen. He gave Jason his customary congratulatory salute for passing the gift of learning milestone.

Red began in earnest. "Jason, life is full of many contradictions. In fact, the longer you live, the more the reality of life will seem like one great paradox. But if you live long enough and search hard enough, you will find a miraculous order to the confusion.

"All of the lessons I am trying to teach you as a part of the ultimate gift I am leaving you through my will are generally learned as people go through their lives facing struggles and problems. Any challenge that does not defeat us ultimately strengthens us.

"One of the great errors in my life was sheltering so many

people—including you—from life's problems. Out of a misguided sense of concern for your well-being, I actually took away your ability to handle life's problems by removing them from your environment.

"Unfortunately, human beings cannot live in a vacuum forever. A bird must struggle in order to emerge from the eggshell. A well-meaning person might crack open the egg, releasing the baby bird. This person might walk away feeling as though he has done the bird a wonderful service when, in fact, he has left the bird in a weakened condition and unable to deal with its environment. Instead of helping the bird, the person has, in fact, destroyed it. It is only a matter of time until something in the bird's environment attacks it, and the bird has no ability to deal with what otherwise would be a manageable problem.

"If we are not allowed to deal with small problems, we will be destroyed by slightly larger ones. When we come to understand this fact, we live our lives not avoiding problems, but welcoming them as challenges that will strengthen us so that we can be victorious in the future."

Red Stevens paused and stared directly into the camera in a way that let us all know his conviction was borne through a life of experience in dealing with problems.

Red continued. "Jason, I cannot turn back the clock and allow you to deal with each of the problems in the past that I eliminated from your life when I should have given you the opportunity to deal with them yourself. If I could take us both back in time, I would, but now I am left with trying to teach you the value of problems, struggles, and obstacles.

"Since you have not had any experience in this area, you will have to learn quickly. There are problems heading your way that you are not prepared for. During the next thirty days, you will begin the preparation.

"This month, I want you to go out and find people with problems in each stage of life. I want you to find a child, a young adult, a full-grown adult, and an older person—each of whom is experiencing a profound problem. Not only are you to find these four individuals, but you must be able to describe to Mr. Hamilton the benefit or the lesson that is derived from each specific situation.

"When we can learn from our own problems, we begin to deal with life. When we can learn from other people's problems, we begin to master life.

"I wish you well, and I hope to talk with you again next month."

Even though the video had ended, Jason continued staring at the blank screen. He rose slowly and walked toward the door. As he opened it, he paused, turned back toward Miss Hastings and me, and said, "I will do my best and call you later."

Then he closed the door behind him.

Miss Hastings turned to me and said, "The process seems

to be beginning to work. I am detecting a shift in his attitude. What do you think?"

"I hope you're right," I responded, "because I have a feeling the road gets steeper the farther we go."

———————

Once again I found myself waiting for Jason's call and hoping he was faring well. I felt the same way I did the first day I sent my son off to kindergarten. With three days left in the month, Jason finally called and set up an appointment with Miss Hastings for the following morning. Miss Hastings told me he had sounded very worried and unsure of himself. All I could do was hope for the best.

The following morning at the appointed hour, Miss Hastings ushered Jason into my office, got him seated, and pulled up a chair for herself. Jason sat silently, and as I looked at him, I had to admit he did seem very quiet and a bit apprehensive.

Finally, I said, "Well, Jason, it's good to see you again. I assume you have a report on your progress."

Jason glanced up at me and said, "I think I do."

He stared down at his hands, which were folded in his lap, and after a long pause, he slowly began. "Well, I knew I had to find people with problems from the four age groups. So I started by looking for a child. After almost two weeks—during which I was unable to find anything—I was so frustrated one afternoon, I just went for a walk in the park.

"I was feeling sorry for myself and considering that after all this work I was going to lose my inheritance and whatever this ultimate gift is that my Uncle Red has for me.

"Finally, I sat at the end of a bench, and I noticed at the other end of the bench there was a young woman watching a little girl playing on the swing. The woman told me she thought the little girl was really amazing, and in my depressed condition, I was not as kind with her as I should have been because I told her that I didn't see anything amazing about her six- or seven-year-old daughter playing on a swing set.

"She told me, 'First of all, I'm not her mother, although I wish I were. Second, she's probably the most amazing person I have ever seen in my life. I am a volunteer at St. Catherine's Hospital. I work in a program where we try to grant special wishes for terminal patients. Emily has a rare form of cancer. She has been through countless operations and has spent probably half her life in hospitals dealing with great pain. When we told her that we could try to make a special wish of hers come true, she said she would like a fun day in the park. We told her that many kids went to Disney World or ball games or the beach, but she just smiled and said, 'That's very nice, but I'd just like to have a fun day in the park.'"

"This woman went on to tell me that Emily had touched everyone in the hospital and had made a real difference in everyone's life. About that time, Emily stopped swinging and slowly walked across the grass and sat between the two of us on the bench. She turned to me with a smile I'll never forget and told me that her name was Emily and that this was her special day in the park. She asked me if this was my special day in the park too. I told her that I didn't think it was, and she laughed and told me that I could share hers with her.

"So, Mr. Hamilton, I spent the rest of the day in the playground with Emily. I realized that she has more courage and joy in her little seven-year-old body than any normal human being could possibly have.

"At the end of the day, she was very tired, and the young lady from the hospital had to take her away in a wheelchair. But, before Emily left, she told me that when she got back to the hospital, she would talk to the nurses and see if they could arrange for me to have a special day in the park too."

Jason paused and looked directly at me. He had a tear in his eye, and I must admit I was fighting to control my composure as well. Miss Hastings retrieved a box of tissues and said something about her seasonal allergies. We all sat in silence and thought about a young girl whose problem could affect us so profoundly.

Finally, Jason cleared his throat, wiped his eye, and continued. "Later that week, I found a middle-aged man walking down the sidewalk in front of my house. He spotted me getting into my car, so he smiled and walked directly over to me. He stuck out his hand and told me his name was Bill Johnson and that my car was one of the most beautiful cars he had ever seen. He told me that he was in the neighborhood doing odd jobs for people and that it would be a privilege to wash a car like mine.

"I asked him why he was out doing odd jobs, and he told me that through a series of corporate cutbacks, both he and his wife had lost their jobs and that they had three young children at home. Both he and his wife were doing anything they could to make ends meet. Apparently, they had gone through their savings, and they were making it just day to day on what they could pick up doing these jobs. I asked him what would happen if he didn't get enough money, and he just smiled and told me that there was always enough, and that the problem had created some interesting situations for their family. They were spending more time together than they had before, and their children had learned the value of money and work.

"He chuckled as he recounted an incident the previous week when they had no food other than a little oatmeal. He said he was just about to give up when he heard his wife explaining to their children that many of the pioneers in the Old West went for days at a time eating nothing but oatmeal. He told me that their two youngest boys would probably want to eat only oatmeal from now on, no matter how much money they ever had."

Jason paused for several moments, searching for the right words, and then he continued, "He went on to tell me about all the wonderful things that he and his wife and family were learning and doing together. He washed my car, and I paid him what he asked. I tried to give him more, but he wouldn't take it.

"Before he left, I told him that I was sorry for his situation. He just laughed that amazing laugh of his and told me that he felt like he was the luckiest man on earth—that in the whole world, he couldn't think of anyone he would want to trade places with.'"

Jason seemed deep in thought and finally said, "You know what's funny, Mr. Hamilton? As he was telling me that there was no one in the world he would trade places with, I was thinking to myself that in a lot of ways I would love to trade places with him.'"

Miss Hastings supplied the three of us with glasses of water. Jason took a sip of his and resumed his report.

"The next day, I was driving past the entrance to a cemetery, and I noticed the largest funeral procession I had ever seen. I didn't think anything of it, and later that day I was passing back the same way, and out of curiosity, I thought I would drive through and ask one of the workers if it had been a celebrity or something. I drove through the cemetery, and the only person I could see was one very old man standing alone by a grave. Since the funeral procession I had seen had been several hours before, I assumed he was there on his own.

"I got out of my car and approached the old gentleman. When he heard me walking up behind him, he turned in my direction. I told him I was sorry for interrupting him, but that earlier in the day when I was driving by, I had seen the largest funeral procession I had ever witnessed. I told him I was just wondering if he might have known if it was a celebrity or superstar or something.

"He laughed softly and told me it had, indeed, been a celebrity and a superstar. He told me he knew that for a fact because he had lived with her for almost sixty years. Apparently, his wife had been a schoolteacher for forty years and had influenced so many of her students that literally hundreds of them had come in from all parts of the country for her funeral. So, he felt that made her a celebrity and a superstar, both.

"I told him I was sorry for disturbing him on what must be the worst day of his life. He just laughed that quiet laugh again and told me that his life would be different, but that no one who lived sixty years with his Dorothy could ever have a bad day. 'I was just standing here thanking Dorothy for everything she had done, and I had just promised her I wouldn't let her down.'"

Jason took another sip of his water, looked at both Miss Hastings and me, and continued. "That old man put his arm around my shoulder, and we walked out of the cemetery together. As I was getting in my car, he told me that if there was ever anything he could do for me that I was to call on him. I just sat in my car and watched him slowly drive away."

Jason seemed to have concluded his report at that point. I waited, but he did not continue, so I finally said, "Jason, you found a child who is living through one of the most difficult problems anyone could face with a joy that it is hard for me to understand. You found a middle-aged man and his family who are dealing with financial crisis while maintaining their sense of family and dignity. You found an older man who has taken a tragedy of death and turned it into a celebration of life. But, Jason, you were to have also found a young person with a problem."

Jason cleared his throat and finally resumed speaking. "Well, Mr. Hamilton, I know I was supposed to find a young person, and during the month I found several possible candidates, but I have to admit to you today that I couldn't find any young person who has learned as much from their problem as I have from mine. I have lived my whole life in a selfish and self-centered fashion. I never realized that real people have real problems. It always seemed that problems happened to people on the news or in the movies or something.

"But, thanks to you and my Uncle Red, I finally realized that I have been sheltered from problems, and that I have never learned the wonderful lessons that the people I met this month are learning. I finally know that joy does not come from avoiding a problem or having someone else deal with it for you. Joy comes from overcoming a problem or simply learning to live with it while being joyful."

Miss Hastings' allergies seemed to be acting up again at that moment, as she was dabbing at her eyes and nose.

Finally, Jason asked, "Do you think it will be okay if I serve as one of the four people I was supposed to learn from this month?"

I assured Jason that it met both the spirit and the letter of Red Stevens' final will and testament.

Jason glanced at his watch and said, "If that's all, I need to hurry to be at another appointment on time."

I told him that would be fine, and as Miss Hastings was showing him to the door, she asked, "Where are you rushing off to, Jason?"

He said, "I have to meet a special friend in front of the swing set at the park. I will see you both tomorrow."

EIGHT

THE GIFT OF FAMILY

*Some people are born
into wonderful families.
Others have to find or create them.
Being a member of a family
is a priceless privilege
which costs nothing but love.*

The following day, Jason Stevens, Miss Hastings, and I gathered in the conference room for our monthly meeting which was becoming a welcomed ritual for me. We sat in our established places. I was lost in thoughts of what the next month might bring as Miss Hastings started the videotape.

Red Stevens greeted Jason warmly. "Hello, and congratulations on learning to value the gift of problems. That lesson will serve you well all the days of your life. You are now entering the sixth month of our one-year remedial lesson in life. This month, you will begin to understand and respect the gift of family.

"Now, Jason, I realize that our family is about as messed up as a family can be, and I accept my full share of responsibility for that. However, the best or the worst family situation can teach us a lesson. We either learn what we want or, unfortunately, we learn what we don't want in life from our families. Out of all the young men in the world, I have selected you. I have asked Mr. Hamilton to undertake this monumental task on my behalf for you because you are my great-nephew. It's hard to understand why that means something, but I want you to know that it does.

"Families give us our roots, our heritage, and our past. They also give us the springboard to our future. Nothing in this world is stronger than the bond that can be formed by a family. That is a bond of pure love that will withstand any pressure as long as the love is kept in the forefront.

"It's important for you to realize that families come in all shapes and sizes. Some very blessed people are able to live their whole lives as part of the families they were born into. Other people, like you, Jason—through a set of circumstances—are left without family other than in name. Those people have to go out and create family.

"I know this seems odd to you, but by the end of this month, I believe you will begin to understand what I am trying to tell you. This month, you, Mr. Hamilton, and Miss Hastings will be going on another trip. You will be meeting people who seem to have no family, and in this way I am hoping you will learn the value that a family can provide.

"At the end of this month, I will ask you to demonstrate to Mr. Hamilton that you know and understand what the gift of family means.

"Mr. Hamilton has all the details for your trip, and assuming you accomplish this objective, I will talk to you next month."

Jason turned to me and said, "I don't suppose you're going to tell me where we're going, what we're going to do, or whom we're going to meet, are you?"

I smiled and said, "All in good time, young man. I have been instructed to tell you only what you need to know and only when you need to know it."

Miss Hastings interrupted. "I believe we have made

arrangements to pick you up at your home at 7:30 in the morning. We will be traveling several hours by automobile. Please be prepared to stay one month in a climate similar to the one which we are enjoying here in Boston."

The next morning, Miss Hastings and I were comfortably installed in the back of a long, black limousine driven by a very large gentleman selected especially for this mission. We pulled up in front of Jason's palatial home, which his great-uncle had purchased for him via a trust fund.

Our driver got out and went to the front door to collect Jason and his luggage. A few moments later, I saw the chauffeur—easily carrying both of Jason's suitcases in one hand—leading Jason toward the car. Jason seemed a bit timid around the giant, and when the back door was opened to let Jason in, he appeared relieved to be in the company of Miss Hastings and me.

"Who in the world is that huge guy?" asked Jason.

Miss Hastings replied cheerily, "Oh, you mean Nathan? He is a very nice young man selected especially for this trip."

"What does that mean?" Jason asked.

Miss Hastings just smiled and sipped on a cup of coffee.

I turned and shook hands with Jason, greeting him. "Good morning, Jason. All will become clear at the appropriate time. For now, I suggest you sit back and relax, and I will tell you some of the details as we approach our destination."

We enjoyed a beautiful drive out of Boston, across eastern

Massachusetts, and into New Hampshire. As we turned north along the coast, I began to explain our trip to Jason.

"Before too long, we will be entering the state of Maine. We will travel several miles into a private forest, and we will arrive at the Red Stevens Home for Boys, where you will be a substitute houseparent for the next month. This will give the resident houseparent an opportunity for a well-deserved vacation and will give you an opportunity to get very well acquainted with thirty-six boys ranging in age from six to sixteen."

Jason stared at me dubiously and said, "I thought I was supposed to be learning about family. How in the world did that old man think I would learn about family from a bunch of orphans?"

"*That old man*, as you so eloquently put it, started this place over thirty years ago and has funded it ever since," I responded. "He knew it inside and out, and I am sure the lesson he has planned for you can be found there. I just hope for your sake you can keep an open mind and find it."

"Well, it doesn't make any sense to me," Jason mumbled.

"Nevertheless, you're in for a unique month, to say the least," I said. "As your great-uncle made me the chairman of the board of this institution upon his death, Miss Hastings and I will spend the month working in the office, dealing with some of the donors, and seeing to next year's budget."

A few moments later, we drove off of the main highway and onto a gravel side road. We passed a rustic sign reading, *Red*

Stevens Home for Boys. Several moments later, our excellent driver, Nathan, guided the limousine to a stop in the middle of a courtyard surrounded by several buildings, including a dining commons, a dormitory, a classroom building, a gymnasium, and an administration building.

Nathan got out of the limousine and opened the rear door for the three of us to get out. As he was getting the luggage out of the trunk, the door to the dormitory burst open, and an entire herd of young boys rushed to Nathan and began to mob him. He picked several of them up in the air, hugged several more, and slapped hands with still others. They were all calling his name and seemed to be terribly excited to see him.

Finally, the enthusiastic greeting seemed to be over when Nathan said in a tone that would be hard to ignore, "Now, men, let's get into our dormitory and make sure everything is squared away, because we have a new houseparent here for the month."

The boys responded immediately and rushed back into their dormitory. Nathan, somehow carrying all the luggage at once without seeming to be burdened down, led us into the dormitory. There were two rows of bunks lining each wall with lockers in between.

Nathan dropped Jason's luggage onto the first bunk and said, "Welcome home. This will be your palace for the next thirty days. Mr. Hamilton and Miss Hastings will be staying in the private apartments connected to the administration building."

Nathan turned back to Jason and said, "I would suggest you get unpacked and settled in. You have a lot of catching up to do."

We all agreed to meet in the dining room in approximately twenty minutes. Nathan showed Miss Hastings and me to the two comfortable apartments adjoining the administration building.

At the agreed upon time, we were all seated at the end of a long table in the dining room. Several dozen boys streamed in and sat at what appeared to be assigned places. They were talking excitedly and seemed to be curious about us as a group of outsiders gathered at the end of their table.

After several moments, Nathan stood to his full height, which was, indeed, impressive. I estimated at least 6 feet, 8 inches. At that point, the boys went silent, and Nathan spoke.

"Boys, as you know, your regular houseparent, Brad, will be on vacation for the next month. Jason Stevens will be filling in for him."

Nathan turned to Jason and said, "Stand up, Jason."

Jason stood slowly, and a chorus of young boys called out in ragged unison, "Hi, Jason."

Jason cleared his throat and stammered, "Hi." Jason sat back down quickly.

Nathan resumed his address to the young boys. "Also, Mr. Hamilton and Miss Hastings will be with us for the next month as well. Some of you will remember them being here during our board of director visits with Mr. Stevens. They are very fine people that we are lucky to have here."

Then Nathan bowed his head and gave thanks for the food. All of the boys followed suit and were polite and respectful throughout the meal.

As we enjoyed our lunch, Jason asked Nathan, "Have you been here before?"

Nathan laughed and responded, "You better believe it. The first time I came here, I was smaller than the smallest kid at this table. I was in and out of a few foster homes, but when I think of the good things from my childhood, they all happened here."

"Do you work here now or something?" Jason asked.

Nathan laughed, which sounded like a low rumble of thunder. "Yes and no," he said. "I guess people would think of my main job as being the tight end for the New England Patriots, but as soon as the season's over, I do whatever I can to be useful around here."

Jason seemed shocked and said, "I'm sorry. I thought you were just a limo driver."

"Well, today I am, and proud to do it," Nathan responded. "Tomorrow I may be the head maintenance man or disciplinarian here. One of the things we learned from Red Stevens when I was growing up is that we all do what needs to be done because it's the right thing to do."

"Well, what am I supposed to do here?" Jason asked.

"I believe Mr. Stevens' instructions through Mr. Hamilton

were to let the boys help you figure out what you're supposed to do here," Nathan answered. "So, if they're done eating, I will take Mr. Hamilton and Miss Hastings to the administration building to discuss next year's budget and let your lessons begin."

Nathan slapped Jason on the back with a giant hand and led Miss Hastings and me from the dining room building. As we were passing through the door, I heard Jason calling to us, "Look, I don't have a clue here. I've never been around any kids."

The young boys around the table all erupted into laughter which could be heard as we walked across the courtyard and into the administration building.

For the next month, Miss Hastings and I did all of the legal and budgetary work required for the coming year. We did have several opportunities each day to look in on Jason, and Nathan told us he would keep us informed.

For the first several days, Jason seemed like a stranger. But, eventually he settled into his duties as father, brother, teacher, and friend to three dozen boys. On the last day, as Nathan was loading our luggage into the limousine, each of the boys came out, one at a time, to tell Jason good-bye. Hugs were exchanged, a few tears were shed, and Jason received a number of gifts which would be considered exceedingly valuable to young boys. I noticed several oddly shaped rocks, a four-leaf clover, and an arrowhead, among other heartfelt offerings.

As Nathan drove us out of the courtyard along the gravel

driveway, Jason was turned in the seat waving to the boys until they were out of sight. We sat in silence until we were well along the highway back to Boston.

Finally, Jason spoke. "You know what's amazing? Not one of those boys has a family, but each of them knew more about a family than I did. I think family is not as much about being related by blood as it is about relating through love."

The limousine horn honked, and Nathan let out a blood-curdling yell which I am sure serves him well on the football field. "You finally got it!" he shouted. "I thought you were pretty useless when you got here, but I knew that if you were related to Red Stevens, we had a chance. You see, you come from a great family, and so do I."

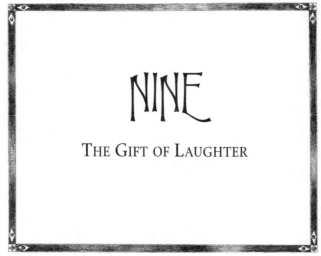

NINE

THE GIFT OF LAUGHTER

Laughter is good medicine for the soul.
Our world is desperately in need
of more such medicine.

When you become an octogenarian, you find yourself dealing with your memories and your mortality. I was sitting in my office thinking of all the wonderful memories I carried with me, and my mind drifted back to Red Stevens.

I had just gotten out of law school and opened my office. The sign on the door read, Hamilton and Associates. The Associates part was more of a wish than a reality, as I spent the majority of each day by myself.

One day, I heard the bell on the outer door ring. I knew that my part-time secretary had already left for the day, so I got up and rushed out to see who it was. There stood a formidable man I later learned was Red Stevens. He told me that he was going to be the biggest oil man and the biggest cattleman in Texas, and he was looking for a good lawyer. He said that he had called the best law school in America and learned that I had graduated first in my class the previous spring.

He just smiled that huge smile I came to know and love, and boomed, "So I thought the best lawyer in the world and the best oil man and cattleman in the world ought to get together."

It didn't seem to bother either of us that I was a lawyer fresh out of law school with no clients, and he was an oil man and a cattleman without any oil or cattle. It began that simply and grew into a longtime professional and personal relationship.

My thoughts of Red were interrupted when Miss Hastings stuck her head into my office and said that Jason Stevens was waiting for us in the conference room.

————————

Red appeared on the video screen and said, "Well, Jason, you've made it through six months of this twelve-month project. I want to remind you that you've come a long way, but you have a long way to go, and if at any point your attitude or your conduct does not meet Mr. Hamilton's expectations, we will end this journey immediately, and you will not receive the ultimate gift, which is the bequest I have left to you in my will.

"This month, you are going to learn about the gift of laughter. The gift of laughter I want you to learn about is not a comedian in a nightclub or a funny movie. It is the ability to look at yourself, your problems, and life in general, and just laugh. Many people live unhappy lives because they take things too seriously. I hope you have learned in the last six months that there are things in life to be serious about and to treasure, but life without laughter is not worth living.

"This month, I want you to go out and find one example of a person who is experiencing difficulties or challenges in his or her life but who maintains the ability to laugh. If a person can laugh in the face of adversity, that individual will be happy throughout life.

"At the end of the month, you will report to Mr. Hamilton

and Miss Hastings about the individual you have found and what you have learned from him or her about the gift of laughter."

Red Stevens began laughing and said, "Someday, Jason, you will have to ask Ted to tell you about some of the laughable situations we got ourselves into in the olden days." As Red continued laughing to himself, the screen went black.

Jason asked, "What is he talking about, Mr. Hamilton?"

I smiled and replied, "That would, indeed, be for another time and another place, but for now, young man, it is time for you to get serious about the gift of laughter."

At that, Miss Hastings walked Jason out of the office.

———————

Our firm's private investigator, Reggie Turner, discreetly followed Jason throughout the month. Reggie reported that Jason seemed to be going about his normal routine and did not appear to be showing any outward signs of exploring the gift of laughter.

On the last day of the month, Miss Hastings buzzed me to say that Jason had called and asked if he could stop by in the afternoon. I told her that would be fine, and she let me know that Jason had informed her he would be bringing someone with him.

At the appointed hour, Miss Hastings escorted Jason into my office along with another young man who was obviously blind. He wore dark glasses and carried a white cane. Miss

Hastings seemed uncomfortable as she watched the blind man walk across the office, and I must admit to feeling a bit of apprehension myself.

"Mr. Hamilton and Miss Hastings," Jason said, "I'd like you to meet David Reese."

Mr. Reese held his hand out and said, "Long time, no see."

It took me a moment to overcome my anxiety and to be able to enjoy his humor. I shook his hand, and we all sat down.

"I met David on a commuter train last week," Jason explained. "We talked during the train trip and several times since, over the phone. He is simply the best example I can imagine of the gift of laughter."

David Reese blurted out, "Yeah, David told me that you guys needed a few laughs around here, so he dragged me in."

David turned his head to the right and said, "Boy, this is really a beautiful office."

"Thank you," I said and was about to tell him about my furnishings when I realized he had been pulling my leg. We all laughed.

I asked Jason, "What was it about this young man that made you believe he had the gift of laughter when you first met him on the train?"

David Reese cut in and answered, "It was my magazine trick, sir."

I smiled and asked, "Okay, what's the magazine trick?"

David Reese explained. "Some of the commuter trains are not

as clean as they should be, so whenever the seats are dusty, people often sit on magazines. Since I can't tell when they're clean and when they're not, I always sit on a magazine. While Jason and I were getting acquainted on the train, a gentleman behind me, as people often do when they're looking for something to read on the train, asked me if I was reading the magazine."

At that point, Jason began laughing out loud and interrupted. "Right after the guy asked David, 'Are you reading that magazine?' David stood up, turned the page, sat back down, and said, 'Yes, sir, but I'll be done before long.'"

When our laughter died down, I asked David how and when he developed the gift of laughter. He explained that he lost his sight early in life and had dealt with many struggles and challenges, not the least of which being people treating him poorly.

"Mr. Hamilton, sometimes in life, either you laugh or you cry," he said. "And I prefer to laugh."

I thought about David Reese and what a wonderful outlook he had on life. His gift of laughter had not only benefited him, but everyone around him, including me. I told Jason that he had certainly fulfilled the assignment for this month.

As Jason walked with David Reese out of the office, David stopped, turned, and said, "Mr. Hamilton, I wanted to tell you before I left—I think that's a beautiful tie you have on."

I was halfway through thanking him for the compliment when I realized he had done it to me again. He and Jason could be heard laughing all the way down the hall to the elevator. Miss Hastings was laughing softly as well.

"So, what are you laughing about?" I finally asked her.

"Well, it is a nice tie," she replied.

TEN

THE GIFT OF DREAMS

Faith is all that dreamers need
to see into the future.

T here are days when you can just feel in your bones that something extraordinary is going to happen. There are other days when the extraordinary things in life surprise you.

As I was waiting for Jason Stevens to arrive for his scheduled appointment, which would begin another month of discovery for both of us, I was standing at my window looking over the Boston skyline and thinking about Red Stevens. It is hard to feel the loss of someone you love when so much of that person remains with you all the time. There are people who have such a huge impact in our lives that they become almost a part of us. Red Stevens had that effect on me, and I know he had the same effect on many others.

There were, indeed, many days I wanted to pick up the phone and hear that gravelly voice with the West Texas accent boom back at me. But, somehow, I knew that I would never be without the good things that Red Stevens had brought into my life.

Red Stevens appeared before us on the large video screen at the end of the conference room. He was, indeed, a great man, and his greatness had manifested itself in every area of his life. Now he was attempting to pass that greatness on to his great-nephew.

"Jason, while you're sitting there, I want to take just a minute to thank Mr. Hamilton and Miss Hastings for agreeing to take on this yearlong project. I hope you'll remember that when you receive the ultimate gift that I have planned for you as my final bequest, the delivery of that gift will be due in large measure to the efforts of my dear friends Theodore Hamilton and Margaret Hastings."

Red seemed so lifelike on the big screen that I wanted to tell him that I was more than glad to do this for him, but I knew it wouldn't do any good to speak those words. Somehow I felt—in my own way—that he would know I was pleased that he had selected me to accompany Jason along this journey.

"Jason, this month you're going to learn about a gift that belongs to all great men and women—the gift of dreams. Dreams are the essence of life—not as it is, but as it can be. Dreams are born in the hearts and minds of very special people, but the fruit of those dreams becomes reality and is enjoyed by the whole world.

"You may not know it, but Theodore Hamilton is known far and wide as the best lawyer in the country. I know that performing at that level was a dream of his when I met him, and he has been living that dream for over fifty years. The dream came true in his heart and mind before it came true in reality.

"I can remember wandering through the swamps of Louisiana, dreaming about becoming the greatest oil and cattle baron in Texas. That dream became such a part of me that when I achieved my goals, it was like going home to a place I had never been before.

"I have been trying to decide, as I have been formulating this ultimate gift for you, which of the gifts is the greatest. If I had to pick one, I think I would pick the gift of dreams because dreams allow us to see life as it can be, not as it is. In that way, the gift of dreams allows us to go out and get any other gift we want out of this life."

Red paused for several moments and seemed to be collecting his thoughts. Then he continued. "Jason, the best way to introduce you to dreams is to acquaint you with some dreamers. I knew many throughout my life. I always considered my friendship with the dreamers to be a treasure.

"One of the first truly great dreamers I ever met in my life had a passion to create places and things that would touch the imagination of people. This passion was with him all the days of his life. He had his share of setbacks and failures as well as many detractors. I never saw him or talked to him at a time when he didn't want to share his latest project with me. He was in the habit of creating huge dream boards that he would hang on the wall and draw out the plans for each of his projects on.

"I remember that when he was on his deathbed, he had arranged to tack the plans for his newest project onto the ceiling of his hospital room. That way, he could continue to look at his dream as he constructed it in his mind.

"A reporter came to visit him while he was in the hospital, and my friend was so weak he could barely talk. So, he actually moved over and asked the reporter to lie on his bed with him so the two of them could look at the plans on the ceiling while my friend shared his dream.

"The reporter was so moved that a person would have that much passion while dealing with a serious illness in the hospital. The reporter concluded his interview, said good-bye to my friend, and left the hospital.

"My friend died later that day.

"Please do not miss the point. A person who can live his entire life with a burning passion for his dream to the extent that he shares it on his deathbed—that is a fortunate person. My friend had his dream with him all the days of his life. It continued to grow and expand. When he would reach one milestone of his dream, another greater and grander one would appear.

"In a real way, my friend taught a lot of people how to dream and imagine a better world. His name was Walt Disney.

"But let me warn you. Your dreams for your life must be yours. They cannot belong to someone else, and they must continue to grow and expand.

"I had another friend whose name you would not know. He said it was his dream to work hard and retire at age fifty. He did, indeed, work hard and achieve a degree of success in his business. He held on to that dream of retiring, but he had no passion beyond that.

"On his fiftieth birthday, a number of us gathered to celebrate both his birthday and his retirement. This should have been one of the happiest days of his life—if his dream had been properly aligned. Unfortunately, his entire adult life had been spent in his profession. That is where he had gained a lot of his pride and self-esteem. When he found himself as a relatively young man without his profession to guide him, he faced the uncertainty of retirement. It was something he thought he had always wanted, but he discovered quickly it created no life-sustaining passion for him.

"A month later, my second friend committed suicide.

"The difference between one dreamer who was still energized by his lifelong passion while on his deathbed and another dreamer whose goal was so ill-fitting for his personality that he committed suicide should be apparent to you.

"Jason, it is important that your dream belong to you. It is not a one-size-fits-all proposition. Your dream should be a custom-fit for your personality, one that grows and develops as you do. The only person who needs to be passionate about your dream is you."

Red Stevens paused, cleared his throat, and seemed to mentally shift gears. He finally continued. "Jason, this month, I want you to begin experiencing the gift of dreams. Assume everything is possible. Make a list of all the things you would like to do and be and have in your life. Then begin to prioritize that list as you discover the ones that generate the most passion in your soul.

"At the end of the month, I want you to share a handful of

those dreams with Mr. Hamilton. There are no right or wrong answers, and keep in mind your dreams will grow and develop through the years. What is more important than the dreams, themselves, is the process of becoming a dreamer.

"I wish you a life of pleasant dreams."

Red Stevens' image faded, and for a moment Jason stared down at his hands, which were folded on the conference room table. Finally he spoke. "I have never thought about what I wanted to do with my life. I guess I always felt that just existing and drifting through day to day was enough."

I stood up and began walking toward the door as I said, "Jason, this would be a good time to start dreaming, and there is no one better to learn the process from than Red Stevens. I look forward to your report at the end of the month."

I walked out of the conference room and left Jason there with his thoughts and—I hoped—his dreams.

———

I will never forget the day, more than three weeks later, that I sat across my desk from Jason Stevens as he shared the beginnings of his lifelong dreams. He began slowly, but gained momentum as he spoke.

"Well, in the beginning I had a huge list of things I thought I wanted to do or be or have. But I realized these weren't really dreams—they were things I could do now if I wanted to. I just hadn't taken the time or energy to do them yet. But when I thought about Walt Disney, several things came to me."

Jason paused for a moment. He looked from Miss Hastings to me and back again. I felt he was seeking encouragement. Miss Hastings smiled and nodded at him, and Jason seemed to gain confidence as he continued.

"Somehow, some way, I would like to be able to help deprived young people live a good life. I don't really mean poor young people. I mean young people who have not learned the power and the passion and the values they can have that will make their lives worth living. Somehow I am going to do for other young people what my Uncle Red is doing for me."

Miss Hastings clapped her hands and replied enthusiastically, "Jason, that's exciting. I can't think of anything better you or anyone else could do with their life."

Jason looked toward me and asked, "Well, does that sound okay to you?"

I smiled and replied, "Jason, after forty years of working with Miss Hastings, I have learned one principle of survival. That is simply to always agree with her. And I do, indeed, agree with her. You have established a most worthwhile dream and goal for your life. Just be sure to remember both of your great-uncle's friends whose stories he shared with you, and keep your dream alive as long as you stay alive."

Miss Hastings walked Jason to the elevator, leaving me alone at my desk. I thought about my dreams and how they were still alive in my eightieth year, although I did vow at that moment to make sure all of my dreams stayed alive and continued to grow.

ELEVEN

THE GIFT OF GIVING

*The only way you can truly get
more out of life for yourself
is to give part of yourself away.*

I was amazed at the progress young Jason Stevens was making as we traveled through our yearlong lesson in life together. He still had a long way to go, but there was definitely a light appearing at the end of the proverbial tunnel.

As we sat at the conference table to begin our ninth month of this journey together, I noticed an amazing change in Jason's countenance, attitude, and demeanor. I felt that he was actually looking forward to whatever Red Stevens had in store for him this month. I knew that I was.

Miss Hastings pressed the appropriate button on the remote control, and Red Stevens appeared once again on the video screen.

"Jason, I want to congratulate you on passing your test as a dreamer. Don't ever think that you have this skill mastered. Your ability to dream and turn those dreams into reality will grow as long as you grow as a person.

"This month, I want you to learn about the gift of giving. This is another one of those paradoxical principles like we talked about several months ago. Conventional wisdom would say that the less you give, the more you have. The converse is true. The more you give, the more you have. Abundance creates the ability to give; giving creates more abundance. I don't mean this simply in financial terms. This principle is true in every area of your life.

"It is important to be a giver and a receiver. Jason, financially, I have given you everything that you have in this world. But, I violated the principle involved in the gift of giving. I gave you money and things out of a sense of obligation, not a true spirit of giving. You received those things with an attitude of entitlement and privilege instead of gratitude. Our attitudes have robbed us both of the joy involved in the gift of giving.

"It is important when you give something to someone that it be given with the right spirit, not out of a sense of obligation. I learned to give to people my whole life. I cannot imagine being deprived of the privilege of giving things and part of myself to other people.

"One of the key principles in giving, however, is that the gift must be yours to give—either something you earned or created or maybe, simply, part of yourself.

"This month, I want you to experience the gift of giving, but if you simply give away the money that I gave you or the things it will buy, we will have once again violated the principle. Therefore, every day for the next thirty days, I want you to give something to someone else that is a gift from you."

"I don't have anything," Jason mumbled.

Red's voice interrupted him. "Now, I know you're probably trying to figure out what in the world you have to give that really came from you. Discovering the things that you already have to give to others will unlock the gift of giving and let you enter into a joyous realm you have never known before. If you are to continue along the path to receiving the ultimate gift I have left you in my will, at the end of this month you will return and report to Mr. Hamilton a gift that you have given each day of this month. As always, I wish you well."

"How in the world am I going to come up with something to

give away every day that didn't come from my Uncle Red?" Jason exploded as the video ended. "Everything I have came from him."

I thought for a minute and then replied, "I knew Red Stevens for more than half a century. He was a tough man but a fair man. He would never demand anything of you that you didn't have the capacity to accomplish."

As Jason slowly walked out of the conference room, I thought about how far he had come, and I hoped the journey would not end at that point.

———— • ————

Throughout that month, I tried to think of things that someone who had been given all his worldly possessions could give away that could actually be called his own. I will admit to having a struggle coming up with a handful of them, and I hoped Jason was doing well on his own. I knew my sense of duty and loyalty to my oldest and dearest friend would oblige me to judge the process fairly.

When Jason returned on the last day of the month, he and Miss Hastings sat across my desk from me. After we had exchanged brief greetings, Jason said, "Look, I want you to know that I did my best, and I'm not sure all of my gifts will fit into whatever Uncle Red had in mind. This wasn't easy."

I smiled and replied, "No lesson worth learning is ever easy."

Jason unfolded a piece of paper and began his report. "It was really tough to come up with thirty things I could give to someone that I didn't get from my great-uncle. But here goes.

"On the first day, I stopped at a shopping center and found a parking space on the first row. As I was getting out of my car, I noticed an elderly couple looking for a space. I backed out and allowed them to park in my space, and I parked in the back of the lot."

Jason looked at me for approval. I simply nodded and said, "Go on."

"On the second day, I got caught downtown in a thunderstorm. I shared my umbrella with a young lady who didn't have one. On the third day, I went to the hospital and donated a pint of blood. On day four, I called a man in my neighborhood who had told me he needed to buy new tires to tell him there was a really good sale going on across town. On day five, I helped an elderly woman carry her packages to her car. On day six, I agreed to watch a neighbor's children for her while she went out with some friends. On day seven, I went to the Center for the Blind and read articles to visually impaired students. On day eight, I served lunch at the soup kitchen, and on day nine I wrote a note and sent a poem to a friend.

"On day ten, I agreed to take my neighbor's kids to school. On day eleven, I helped box and move donated items for the Salvation Army. On days twelve and thirteen, I let some visiting foreign exchange students stay in my home. On day fourteen, I helped a local Scout troop with their weekly meeting. On day fifteen, I found a man with a dead battery and jump-started his car. On day sixteen, I wrote letters for several people who were in the hospital. On day seventeen, I went to the local animal shelter and walked several of their dogs in the park. On day eighteen, I gave the frequent flyer miles I had earned with an airline to a high school band group planning a trip to a parade in California. Day nineteen, I worked with a local service organization and delivered meals to disabled and elderly people.

"Days twenty, twenty-one, twenty-two, and twenty-three, I took a group of inner-city kids who had never been camping and fishing on a trip with the Scout troop. I had never been camping or fishing either. On day twenty-four, I helped a local church with their rummage sale. Days twenty-five and twenty-six, I worked with a crew on a Habitat for Humanity house. Day twenty-seven, I let a local charity group use my home for a reception. Day twenty-eight, I helped one of my neighbors rake the leaves out of his yard. Day twenty-nine, believe it or not, I helped to bake cookies for the elementary school's bake sale."

Jason stopped his report at that point. I couldn't imagine he had gone through twenty-nine days of giving only to fail on the thirtieth day. Finally, feeling alarmed, I asked, "And what about day thirty, Jason?"

Jason laughed and said, "Today is day thirty, and I would like both you and Miss Hastings to have some of my homemade cookies from the bake sale."

Jason reached into a bag I had not noticed at his feet and gave us each some of the cookies.

I felt a sense of relief that Jason had completed his task for the month. I took a bite of one of his cookies and responded, "Not too bad, but I'm glad that your dream does not involve a lot of baking."

We all laughed, and Jason talked well into the afternoon about all the people he had met and given part of himself to throughout the month. I was reminded of how a small gift when it is given can be a magnificent gift as it is received.

During the first month of this process because I was angry and resentful like every... I realized an inheritance like ever... in my family, when Uncle Rea... I was further illustrated by... about... what I thoughts of... a crazy... when for the ent... knew... as happening... myself learned about... with Gus Casse... as down...

At that time... when Gus ora... big post holes and... a fence. too the furthest thing... my mind. But now, looking back... I realize... that Gus' love for... Uncle Red was being passed on to me... he loved me enough to make sure that... I learned the entire lesson that Uncle... learned... for the gift of work... which come... there is a kind... from doing a job well.

During the month when I lear... about the gift of money, I discou... having a bad or indifferent att... about money leads to a hollow... existence. It's when you lear... love people and use money...

...that if I c... ...four dollars, left to live...

TWELVE

THE GIFT OF GRATITUDE

*In those times when we yearn
to have more in our lives,
we should dwell on the things
we already have. In doing so,
we will often find that our lives
are already full to overflowing.*

A s Jason arrived for our tenth monthly meeting together, I was still marveling at how he had found enough gifts within himself to give away something every day of the previous month. I thought of all the lessons we had learned, and I was reminded of the fact that we just had a few months to go to complete Red Stevens' ultimate gift to Jason.

I had the feeling that is described by baseball pitchers who are close to completing a no-hit game: You realize that one minor mistake at any point can ruin the entire effort. As Jason completed each monthly task, I think we both felt a sense of accomplishment but, at the same time, a realization that we had more to lose than ever before.

As Miss Hastings, Jason, and I gathered in the conference room, I think we were all anxious to find out what Red Stevens had in store for us. Miss Hastings started the video, and the familiar image of Red Stevens appeared before us.

"Greetings to you all, and my congratulations to Jason, and thanks to Mr. Hamilton and Miss Hastings."

Red Stevens then winked his right eye, which was a gesture I had enjoyed for over five decades. That wink could speak a myriad of emotions, and I never thought I would see it again after attending his funeral.

"When you prepare your will and a video like this, you automatically have to think about your entire life," he continued. "I have been so many places and experienced so many things, it is hard to remember that I have only lived one lifetime.

"I remember as a young man, being so poor that I had to do day labor for food to eat, and had to sleep along the side of the road. I also remember being in the company of kings and presidents and knowing all of the material things this life has to offer. As I look back, I am thankful for it all.

"During what, at the time, I considered to be some of my worst experiences, I gained my fondest memories."

Red paused, collected his thoughts, and pressed on. "Jason, this month, you are going to learn a lesson that encompasses something that has been totally lacking in your life. That is gratitude.

"I have always found it ironic that the people in this world who have the most to be thankful for are often the least thankful, and somehow the people who have virtually nothing, many times live lives full of gratitude.

"While still in my youth, shortly after going out on my own to conquer the world, I met an elderly gentleman who today would be described as homeless. Back then, there were a lot of people who rode the rails, traveling throughout the country doing just a little bit of work here and there in order to get by. It was during the Depression, and some of these so-called hobos or tramps were well educated and had lives full of rich experiences.

"Josh and I traveled together for almost a year. He seemed very old at that time, but since I was still in my teens, I may have had a faulty perspective. He is one of the only people I ever met of whom I could honestly say, 'He never had a bad day.' Or if he did, there was certainly no outward sign of it. Traveling about as we did, we often found ourselves wet, cold, and hungry. But Josh never had anything but the best to say to everyone we met.

"Finally, when I decided to settle down in Texas and seek my fortune there, Josh and I parted company. Settling down was simply not a priority in his life. When we parted, I asked him why he was always in such good spirits. He told me that one of the great lessons his mother had left him was the legacy of the Golden List.

"He explained to me that every morning before he got up, he would lie in bed—or wherever he had been sleeping—and visualize a golden tablet on which was written ten things in his life he was especially thankful for. He told me that his mother had done that all the days of her life, and that he had never missed a day since she shared the Golden List with him.

"Well, as I stand here today, I am proud to say I haven't missed a day since Josh shared the process with me almost sixty years ago. Some days, I am thankful for the most trivial things, and other days I feel a deep sense of gratitude for my life and everything surrounding me."

Red cleared his throat, took a sip of water, gathered himself, and continued. "Jason, today, I am passing the legacy of the Golden List on to you. I know that it has survived well over one hundred years simply being passed from Josh's mother through Josh to me, and now to you. I don't know how Josh's mother discovered the process, so its origins may go back much further than I know.

"In any event, I am passing it on to you, and if you will be diligent in the beginning, before long it will simply become a natural part of your life, like breathing.

"This month, I want you to think about all of the things you have to be thankful for. And when you return at the end of the month, you are to share your version of the Golden List with Mr. Hamilton. I hope you will continue the process for the rest of your life, and someday you will have the privilege—as I now have—of sharing the legacy again."

Red's image faded away, leaving the screen blank.

The next morning, as is my usual habit, I woke up precisely at 5:00 a.m. I have done this for years without the aid of an alarm clock. I lay there thinking about the Golden List that Red had shared with Jason, and I began to construct my own list in my mind before I got out of bed.

As an eighty-year-old, it takes me more time to get out of bed than it used to, so I knew from that point on, I would have plenty of time each day for Red Stevens' exercise in gratitude.

As the end of the month approached, my thoughts were drawn to Jason Stevens. I hoped he was progressing with the Golden List each day as I was. I was concerned because he had spent his whole life taking everything for granted.

Jason arrived a bit early on the last day of the month, and he had a gleam in his eye and a spring in his step. My concerns began to fade just a bit. Jason and I shook hands, and he greeted Miss

Hastings. I sat behind my desk, and Jason helped Miss Hastings with her chair and then dropped into the vacant one beside her.

"Well, you seem to be in a good mood today, Jason," I observed.

He laughed aloud and responded, "I have more reasons than I ever imagined to be in a good mood."

Then he began to share his Golden List.

"Each day this month, I have been thinking about things I am grateful for. I never would have imagined that there are so many.

"First, I am thankful for my health. I have always had my health, and over the last ten months, through the directives of Uncle Red's will, I have met several people who have physical problems. So I will always be grateful for my good health.

"Second, I am thankful for my youth. I have learned that I have missed many of the important things in life thus far; however, I feel that youth can overcome any obstacle.

"Third, I am thankful for my home. It's a wonderful home, made possible through my Uncle Red's generosity. I never really appreciated it as I should, but through this ultimate gift from the will, I have been able to share my home with other people and have come to appreciate it myself.

"Fourth, I am thankful for my friends." He looked toward Miss Hastings and me, then continued. "Including both of you, Brian, Gus Caldwell, the boys at the Red Stevens Home, and—in a special way that is hard to explain—my Uncle Red.

"Fifth, I am thankful for my education. Although I did not

apply myself well during college, it did give me the tools I need to go out and make education and learning a real part of my life.

"Sixth, I am thankful for all of the places I have been able to travel to and experience throughout the years thanks to my Uncle Red.

"Seventh, I am thankful for my car. It is fun as well as dependable and reliable. I learned from my friend Brian that everyone isn't as lucky as I am.

"Eighth, I am thankful for my family. Although I have not always appreciated them throughout the years, I have learned enough about families to know that, in the future, I can get along better with the family I have and at the same time create family relationships with new people.

"Number nine, I am grateful for the money that my Uncle Red has made possible over the years. But even more than that, I am grateful for the fact that, through my Uncle Red's efforts, I have learned the value and use of money. I look forward to learning more about the subject in the future and handling the money I have more wisely.

"And finally, number ten, I am thankful for each of the steps leading up to the ultimate gift. I am thankful to my Uncle Red for thinking of me as he went to the trouble of putting it together, and I am grateful to both of you for carrying out his wishes."

Miss Hastings broke in and said, "Jason, that is a marvelous list. I think you have done very well in understanding the Golden List and the gift of gratitude."

Jason smiled and remarked, "What's really amazing, Miss Hastings, is that I could go on and on. There are so many things that each of us has to be grateful for, it is hard to limit it to only ten."

I congratulated Jason, and we all shook hands as he parted. I reminded myself to be sure that Red Stevens and Jason were both on my Golden List the next morning as I thought of all the things for which I was grateful.

THIRTEEN

The Gift of a Day

*Life at its essence boils down
to one day at a time.
Today is the day!*

As we entered the eleventh month of Jason Stevens' pursuit of the ultimate gift, I realized that during this month we would pass the one-year anniversary of Red Stevens' death. My thoughts were often of my longtime friend and companion.

Red Stevens and I had come from two totally different worlds, and outwardly we had seemed to have very little in common. But somewhere, we had found a point of common ground between us that enabled us both to develop and nurture a friendship through five decades.

I will always remember Red Stevens as being bigger than life. While I felt comfortable in the confines of my office in Back Bay Boston, Red Stevens always seemed at home in Texas. Somehow, it seemed to fit him. It takes a place like Texas to build men like Red Stevens.

I had heard it said before that no one is ever alone if he or she has just one friend. I came to believe that no one could be alone if he or she ever had a friend like Red Stevens. I knew he would always be with me. I felt pride and responsibility that he had selected me to accompany Jason through each step of the journey toward the ultimate gift Red had planned for him.

These thoughts were in my mind when Jason Stevens arrived, and we settled into those familiar places in our law firm's conference room. Right on cue, Red Stevens came to us once again via the videotape and the large screen at the end of the room.

He smiled and boomed, "Congratulations, Jason. Since I am

talking to you today, I know that Mr. Hamilton approved of your handling of the gift of gratitude last month.

"Jason, I want you to know that as I was contemplating the ultimate gift I wanted to present you through my will, I spent a lot of time thinking about you. I think you gained a permanent place in my Golden List each morning. I am thankful that you and I share a family heritage, and I sense a spark in you that I have always felt in myself. We are somehow kindred spirits beyond just our family ties."

Out of the corner of my eye, I could see Jason nodding his head as Red spoke.

Red continued. "As I have been going through the process of creating my will and thinking about my life and my death, I have considered all of the elements in my life that have made it special. I have reviewed many memories, and I carry them with me like a treasure.

"When you face your own mortality, you contemplate how much of life you have lived versus how much you have left. It is like the sand slipping through an hourglass. I know that at some point I will live the last day of my life. I have been thinking about how I would want to live that day or what I would do if I had just one day left to live. I have come to realize that if I can get that picture in my mind of maximizing one day, I will have mastered the essence of living, because life is nothing more than a series of days. If we can learn how to live one day to its fullest, our lives will be rich and meaningful.

"Jason, during the next thirty days, I want you to plan how you would live the last day of your life. And at the end of the month, I want you to give the details to Mr. Hamilton. I think you will discover how much life can be packed into one simple day, and then I hope you will discover the same thing I have discovered. Why should we wait until the last day of our lives to begin living the maximum day?

"You have all of the tools and elements you will need to design this last day for yourself. I wish you well today and every day of the rest of your life."

Red Stevens vanished from the screen.

Jason let out a deep sigh and said, "You know, I've never really thought about dying or the last day of my life."

I smiled and responded, "When I was your age, I didn't think about it much, either, but I think what your great-uncle is trying to teach you is that there is a lot to be gained by thinking through the process; and I believe the younger you are when you learn this lesson, the more quality you will have in your life."

Jason and I rose and shook hands, and he left to go about his month of discovery in the realm of the gift of a day.

Unlike Jason, I had, indeed, thought quite a bit about how I might spend the last day of my life, and all of the things I would want to pack into that one twenty-four-hour period. These thoughts were much on my mind throughout the entire month.

———————

At the end of the month, Jason Stevens entered my office with the demeanor and carriage of a man on a mission. He sat down in one of my client chairs, and Miss Hastings took the other.

"Jason, it is wonderful to see you again," I said, "and I hope the month has been fruitful for you."

"It has been great," Jason blurted out excitedly, "but I'm not sure a day is long enough to cram in all the things I would want to do before I die. What I found to be amazing is the fact that the things I would most want to accomplish on the last day of my life are really simple and ordinary things.

"When I first started thinking about the process, I thought I would want to climb a great mountain or create some wonderful art or something. But after much thought, I have come to realize that my perfect day would be filled with the best of simple things."

Jason paused and looked at both Miss Hastings and me. He reached into his jacket pocket and drew out a single sheet of paper. He glanced at his notes and began again.

"Well, on the last day of my life, I would like to wake up early in the morning—there is certainly no time to waste. Before even getting out of bed, I would go through all of the things I am grateful for and create my mental Golden List. But unlike the list we talked about last month with ten things, I think on the last day of my life I would have to add many more things to the list for which I am thankful.

"I would like to have an early breakfast outdoors on a patio or balcony with a group of very special friends. I would tell them how much they mean to me, and I would want to give them each a gift that would be the recipe for getting the most out of their days and, therefore, their entire lives.

"After breakfast, I would want to call a number of people who have been special to me—people like Gus Caldwell in Texas, the people at the Red Stevens Library in South America, all of the boys at the home up in Maine, and many others. I would also want to call all of my relatives and other people with whom I have not had a good relationship. I would want to tell each of them I am sorry for whatever has gone wrong between us, and I would want to ask them to do what I am doing, which is simply hold on to all the good memories and release all the bad ones.

"For lunch, I would like to take my friend Brian to his favorite restaurant and buy him anything he wanted. I would ask him to share with me the dreams he has for his life.

"During the afternoon, I would like to enjoy some of the simple pleasures, including a walk in the park—hopefully with the little girl named Emily I met earlier this year—followed by a trip to the art museum and a brief outing on a sailboat around Boston Harbor.

"Then, in the evening, I would like to have a special banquet for all of my friends and their friends, and I certainly would want both of you there. At the end of the banquet, I would like to step up on a platform and share with everyone the gifts that my great-uncle, Red Stevens, left to me. I would want to have it videotaped so that my dream of sharing this wonderful gift with other young people like me could go on after I died."

Jason glanced up at Miss Hastings and me, and then back down to his sheet of paper. After several moments, he folded the paper and put it back into his jacket pocket. "Well, there are many other things I thought of to do, and they're all good," he said, "but those are the ones I thought I could fit into my last day."

I smiled and responded, "Jason, I can't think of any better way to spend one's last day. I think we can all agree that you have come to a wonderful understanding of what your Uncle Red had in mind in the gift of a day."

Jason stood and shook my hand warmly and actually gave Miss Hastings a brief hug. As she escorted him to the elevator, I couldn't help but remember the sullen, angry young man who had come into my office just one year earlier. I knew that Red Stevens was smiling down on us.

FOURTEEN

THE GIFT OF LOVE

Love is a treasure
for which we can never pay.
The only way we keep it
is to give it away.

I must admit to having mixed emotions as I awaited Jason Stevens' arrival for what I knew would be the beginning of our last monthly journey together in this yearlong odyssey of discovery. I was elated about the progress Jason had made, and I felt confident and excited about the future he had before him; but I was also struck with the sense of loss that comes at the end of any difficult but meaningful journey.

I felt, in a way, as if I would be losing my longtime friend, Red Stevens, once again because I would not be able to look forward to these monthly visits. On the other hand, if I had learned anything from going through this transformation with Jason, it was a fact that the best of Red Stevens would always be with me.

Miss Hastings called me on the intercom to let me know that Jason Stevens had arrived. I met them in the conference room, and I believe they both, in a way, were sharing the same mixed emotions I felt.

Miss Hastings performed her now familiar ritual of taking the videotape from the box Red Stevens had left in our vault along with his will. She put the tape in the video player at the end of our conference room.

Red Stevens' image appeared on the large screen, and knowing him as well as I did, I believed he was feeling some of the same emotions we all shared.

Red began. "Jason, I want to congratulate you for making it to the last step of the ultimate gift I planned for you. I am very proud that you obviously made it through the learning process involved in the gift of a day from last month. I do not know what you planned for your last day, but I know it was judged acceptable by Mr. Hamilton. I would imagine that the activities you planned for the day were much like mine—very simple and somewhat ordinary.

"If we are living our lives the way we should, everything should be in such an order that we wouldn't change the last day of our life from any other day. Please always remember that none of us is guaranteed a long life. We're not guaranteed anything but today.

"Also, I think if you will consider it, you will realize that there is probably nothing that you would plan for your last day of life that you couldn't do today or tomorrow. Somehow, I think life's tragedies are made up not as much of the great failures as much as of the simple pleasures and kind gestures missed."

Red Stevens paused, and I could feel his emotions and all of ours as we sat in the darkened conference room.

Finally, he continued. "Jason, in this last month, I'm going to introduce you to the one part of my ultimate gift to you that encompasses all of the other gifts as well as everything good you will ever do, have, or know in your life. That is the gift of love.

"Anything good, honorable, and desirable in life is based on love. Anything bad or evil is simply life without the love involved. Love is a misused and overused term in our society. It is applied to any number of frivolous things and pursuits; but the love I am talking about in the gift of love is the goodness that comes only from God. Not everyone believes or acknowledges that. And that's okay. I still know that real love comes from Him—whether or not we know it.

"Since love is a part of each of the other gifts you have experienced throughout this year, during the next thirty days, I want you to explore how love is involved in all the other gifts, and prepare to share what you find with Mr. Hamilton.

"Please remember that your attitude and your performance are still being judged, and if you fail—even in the twelfth month—you will not be receiving the entire ultimate gift I have planned for you. My warning to you is not meant to be threatening, but holding you to the highest standard in my own way is the greatest act of love I can show you."

Red Stevens' image faded, and the screen was, once again, dark.

Jason sat motionless for several minutes. I knew that he was deep in thought. Finally, we all stood and quietly left the conference room. It was almost as if we had been to a memorial service for Red Stevens. I felt it was a fitting tribute to my oldest and dearest friend.

——— ———

On the last day of the month, Miss Hastings ushered Jason into my office. They both sat in their familiar places, and we exchanged brief greetings. I could tell that Jason had much on his mind.

"Mr. Hamilton and Miss Hastings," Jason began, "I do not have the words to express what this process over the last year has meant to me. I am simply not the same person I was a year ago. I feel that, in many ways, today is my birthday. I want to thank you both for being a part of it."

I noticed that Jason's eyes seemed moist, and Miss Hastings' seasonal allergies seemed to act up at that very moment. I will admit to feeling a lump in my own throat. Jason took a deep breath and launched into his report.

"During the first month of this year, I was angered and very resentful of not receiving an inheritance like everyone else in the family. I was further frustrated when I learned about what I thought then was a crazy plan for the entire year. Then I found myself learning about the gift of work with Gus Caldwell down in Texas.

"At that time, love was the furthest thing from my mind when Gus Caldwell ordered me to dig post holes and build a fence. But as I look back on it, I realize that Mr. Caldwell had a great love for my Uncle Red and passed that on to me. He loved me enough to make sure that I learned the entire lesson that my Uncle Red planned for the gift of work. I also learned that there is a certain love which comes from doing a job well. When you can step back at the end of a long, hard day and watch the sun set over a straight and strong fence that you built yourself, you get the feeling that everything is right with the world.

"During the month when I learned about the gift of money,

I learned that loving money leads to a hollow, empty existence. But when you learn how to love people and use money, everything is in its proper perspective.

"From the gift of friends, I learned that you can love others in a way I had never known. When you just worry about yourself, you are always disappointed. But when you think about others and their well-being first, everything works out best for you and for them.

"From the gift of learning, I discovered that people who have no material things—but a passion to learn and a true love of learning—are really quite wealthy. This love for knowledge has come into my life, and I cannot believe that I was so self-centered that I ignored the wisdom of the ages as I pursued my own self-destruction.

"The gift of problems taught me that obstacles are nothing more than a challenge that we face. Before this year, I looked at problems as something that was totally bad, something that had to be dealt with—or, better yet, ignored. But when you look at your problems through a spirit of love, you realize that there is a grand design to this world, and the problem is given to you for the lesson it will teach you and the better person it will make you.

"From the gift of family, I learned that families are present when love is present. People can become a family when they add love to their relationships. Without love, families are just a group of people who share the same family tree.

"The gift of laughter taught me that in order to love life, you have to enjoy it. And when you can laugh at the good things and the bad, you will begin to feel the love life really has to offer.

"During my exploration of the gift of dreams, I came to understand that life has been given to us with a sense of love for everything around us. Our passions and dreams and goals are the outward manifestations of the love we feel inside.

"Before I experienced the gift of giving, I thought that if you gave something away, someone else now possessed it, and you were left with less than you had before. In reality, when you give out of love, both the giver and the receiver have more than they started with.

"The gift of gratitude taught me that we can truly feel and experience love when we remember and enjoy all of the wonderful things we have been given.

"And, finally, from the gift of a day, I learned that if I only had twenty-four hours left to live, I would want to feel and experience as much love as I could and pass it on to as many others as possible."

Jason paused and cleared his throat. I was just about to tell him that I heartily approved of his mastery of the gift of love, when he continued.

"If I were going to really try to define the gift of love in tangible terms, I would have to cite as an example what my Uncle Red did for me and what he gave me during this last year. When we truly love others, our love makes each of us a different person, and it makes each one we love a different person too.

"My Uncle Red's love for me in giving me the ultimate gift forever changed my life and who I am."

Jason rose to his feet and hugged Miss Hastings. He stepped around my desk and hugged me as well. He thanked us both for everything and let us know that he looked forward to staying in touch with us in the future.

As Jason put his hand on the doorknob, I stopped him by saying, "Just a minute, Jason. There is one more step in the ultimate gift that you don't know about."

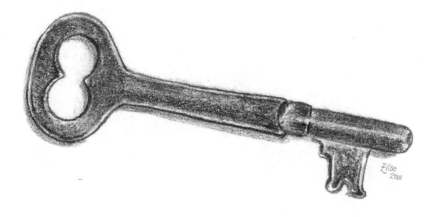

FIFTEEN

THE ULTIMATE GIFT

In the end,
life lived to its fullest
is its own ultimate gift.

J ason turned with a bewildered look on his face and said, "I don't know what you're talking about, Mr. Hamilton. We did all twelve of the gifts that Uncle Red mentioned, and he said that this month would be the last one."

"Well, as Red Stevens' attorney and as executor of his estate," I replied, "I can tell you that he had one last bequest in his will that would only be made available if all the conditions were met. As the sole arbiter of each of the conditions, I can tell you that they have all been met and exceeded."

Jason continued to appear perplexed and said, "I really don't know what you are talking about. I thought—"

Miss Hastings interrupted and said, "I realize you thought you were done. But there is one more step. If you'll follow me into the conference room, I do believe all things will become clear."

We adjourned to the conference room, and in a few moments, Red Stevens was once again speaking to us from the video screen.

"Jason," he said, "I want to tell you how proud of you I am. You have completed each element and received each part of the ultimate gift I had planned for you. I wish that I had come into possession of all twelve gifts as early in life as you have. Now that you have received the ultimate gift, not only do you have the privilege of enjoying it, but you have the responsibility of living your life to its fullest with each gift in balance. You have the further responsibility of passing along the ultimate gift whenever it is possible.

"I wish I could be with you to simply watch the wonderful things that are going to happen in your life, but somehow—in my own way—I suspect I will be with you.

"Jason, I have done a lot of things in my life, but the best of them may well be passing the ultimate gift on to you. Please don't let me down. Make the gift grow and be fruitful. Make your life an extension of the ultimate gift you have received. If you will do all of these things, you will have—in your own way—given to me your version of the ultimate gift."

The image of Red Stevens faded away for what would be the last time.

As the lights came up, Jason leaped to his feet and, with a confident look on his face, said, "I am going to do it! I am going to use every element of the ultimate gift, and I am going to find a way to pass it on to deprived people who are as I was a year ago. I had no idea that the greatest gift anyone could be given is the awareness of all of the gifts he or she already has. Now I know why God made me and put me on this earth. I understand the purpose for my life and how I can help other people find their purpose."

Jason, once again, headed for the door, and, once again, I stopped him—this time by saying, "Young man, I have never seen anybody in such a hurry to leave."

Jason turned around with that same bewildered expression on his face. "I'm sorry, Mr. Hamilton," he said, "I just thought—"

"I know, you thought we were done," I interrupted. "If you will just sit back down, I will discharge my final duty with regard to Red Stevens' last will and testament."

Miss Hastings handed me the voluminous document, and I turned to the appropriate page. I was just getting my reading glasses out of my pocket when Jason blurted out, "I just thought—"

I interrupted Jason again by scolding him playfully, "Young man, never interrupt a duly appointed attorney when he is trying to discharge his final duty."

Miss Hastings laughed and added, "Especially when the attorney is eighty years old."

We all laughed together, and I read from the document. "And to my great-nephew, Jason Stevens, I leave control of my charitable trust fund. Its current value is somewhere slightly over $1 billion. As my great-nephew has shown himself to be responsible and able in every area of life, he will have the sole control of this charitable trust fund which supports the Red Stevens Home for Boys, the Red Stevens Library Program, several scholarship programs, hospitals, and many other worthy institutions.

"I direct Jason to use the wisdom and experience he has gained as a recipient of the ultimate gift to manage these projects and any others that he deems significant."

Jason sat back in his chair, totally stunned. Finally, after several false starts, he said, "Do you mean that I am in charge of all of those things?"

I gave him a formal look and tone, answering, "As I read the document, it would seem to be the case. You are in charge of all of the aforementioned, and anything else you feel to be important."

Jason lit up. A smile spread across his face. He looked toward Miss Hastings and back to me, saying, "I could use part of the charitable trust to spread the ultimate gift all around the world."

Miss Hastings replied, "If I'm not mistaken, I believe that's what Red Stevens had in mind all along."

Jason hugged both of us again, thanked us profusely, and parted.

Miss Hastings and I sat back down at the conference room table and simply drank in the feeling of elation and success.

"Did you notice," she observed, "that he never asked about his income or wages or anything else like that?"

I nodded with a smile, as we both reflected on the amazing transformation that Jason had made in one year.

Finally, ever vigilant Miss Hastings left the conference room to complete her many duties for the day. I was left alone in the conference room, and I couldn't resist rewinding the videotape and watching Red Stevens' last message one more time.

When it was over, I spoke to the darkened screen. "Well, old friend, I believe this is where we finally do part company. I wish I could tell you how thankful I am to be included in the ultimate gift, and I wish I could tell you all of the wonderful things Jason has done and is going to do."

As I walked out of the conference room, I realized Red did know and—in his own way—would be watching with me as Jason lived out and passed on The Ultimate Gift.

ABOUT THE AUTHOR

Jim Stovall is among the most sought-after motivational speakers anywhere. Despite failing eyesight and eventual blindness, Jim Stovall has been a national champion Olympic weight lifter, a successful investment broker, and an entrepreneur. He is the cofounder and president of the Narrative Television Network, which makes movies and television accessible for America's 13 million blind and visually impaired people and their families. Although NTN was originally designed for the blind and visually impaired, more than 60 percent of its nationwide audience is made up of fully sighted people who simply enjoy the programming. The network's programming is also available free of charge, 24 hours a day, via the Internet at www.NarrativeTV.com.

Jim Stovall hosts the network's talk show, *NTN Showcase*. His guests have included Katharine Hepburn, Jack Lemmon, Carol Channing, Steve Allen, and Eddie Albert, as well as many others. The Narrative Television Network has received an Emmy Award and an International Film and Video Award among its many industry honors.

It has grown to include more than 1,200 cable systems and broadcast stations, reaching more than 35 million homes in the United States, and it is shown in 11 foreign countries.

Jim Stovall joined the ranks of Walt Disney, Orson Welles, and four U.S. presidents when he was selected as one of the Ten Outstanding Young Americans by the U.S. Junior Chamber of Commerce in 1994. He has appeared on Good Morning America and CNN, and has been featured in *Reader's Digest*, *TV Guide*, and *Time* magazines. He is the author of previous books titled *You Don't Have To Be Blind To See, Success Secrets of Super Achievers,* and *The Way I See The World*. The President's Committee on Equal Opportunity selected Jim Stovall as the 1997 Entrepreneur of the Year. In June 2000, Jim Stovall joined notables such as President Jimmy Carter, Nancy Reagan, and Mother Teresa when he received the International Humanitarian Award.

Jim Stovall can be reached at 918-627-1000.